The Maths We Need Now: Demands, deficits and remedies

Edited by
Clare Tikly and Alison Wolf

Bedford Way Papers

INSTITUTE OF
EDUCATION
UNIVERSITY OF LONDON

First published in 2000 by the Institute of Education, University of London,
20 Bedford Way, London WC1H 0AL
www.ioe.ac.uk

Pursuing Excellence in Education

© Institute of Education, University of London 2000

British Library Cataloguing in Publication Data:
A catalogue record for this publication is available from the British Library

ISBN 0 85473 616 6

Design and typography by Joan Rose
Cover design by Tim McPhee
Page make-up by Cambridge Photosetting Services, Cambridge

Production services by
Book Production Consultants plc, Cambridge

Printed by Watkiss Studios Ltd, Biggleswade, Beds

Contents

0223859

This book is due for return on or before the last date shown below.

2 9 OCT 2003

0 2 FEB 2004

2 0 FEB 2004

2 9 MAR 2004

2 0 MAY 2004

1 5 SEP 2004

1 2 NOV 2004

2 5 FEB 2005

1 0 MAY 2005

0 5 OCT 2005

0 3 JAN 2006

1 8 APR 2006

2 8 APR 2006

1 8 JUL 2006

1 0 NOV 2006

0 4 DEC 2006

0 3 JAN 2007

2 0 FEB 2007

2 6 MAR 2007

- 2 MAY 2007

1 1 DEC 2007

0 4 FEB 2008

3 0 NOV 2009

The Bedford Way Papers Series

Acknowledgements

The chapters in this volume bring together findings from a wide range of studies conducted by the authors in recent (and not so recent) years. In addition to the funders of specific studies, who are acknowledged at different points in the pages that follow, we would like to express our appreciation of the valuable comments offered by the external reviewer and of general support from our home institutions, past and present: the Institute of Education, University of London; the University of Bristol; the London School of Economics and Political Science; the University of Newcastle; the University of Warwick; and City University.

Final preparation of this text (and especially the tables and figures) was undertaken by Angela Barclay and Magdalen Meade; and we are extremely grateful for their assistance and expertise. Our thanks, too, to Geoff Woodhouse, without whom the book would never have been conceived.

Abbreviations

ACAS	Advisory, Conciliation and Arbitration Service
ALBSU	Adult Literacy and Basic Skills Unit
BSA	Basic Skills Agency
BTEC	Business and Technician Education Council
CPVE	Certificate of Pre Vocational Education
CSE	Certificate of Secondary Education
DVE	Diploma in Vocational Education
GCSE	General Certificate of Secondary Education
GNVQs	General National Vocational Qualifications
HESA	Higher Education Statistics Agency
IEA	International Association for the Evaluation of Educational Achievement
ICT	information and communications technology
IT	information technology
ITT	initial teacher training
LEA	local education authority
NAEP	National Assessment of Educational Progress
NCDS	National Child Development Study
NCES	National Center for Education Statistics
NCVQ	National Council for Vocational Qualifications
NVQ	National Vocational Qualification
NFER	National Foundation for Educational Research in England and Wales
NIESR	National Institute of Economic and Social Research
OECD	Organization for Economic Cooperation and Development
OFSTED	Office for Standards in Education
PGCE	Postgraduate Certificate of Education
QCA	Qualifications and Curriculum Authority
QTS	qualified teacher status
SATs	Standardized Assessment Tasks
SCAA	School Curriculum and Assessment Authority
SMILE	School Mathematics Independent Learning Experience
SMP	School Mathematics Project
TIMSS	Third International Mathematics and Science Study
TTA	Teacher Training Agency

1 The State of Mathematics Education

Clare Tikly and Alison Wolf
Mathematical Sciences Group, Institute of Education, University of London

Introduction

Mathematics matters. It matters to individuals and it matters to societies. Indeed, as we enter the twenty-first century, it matters more than ever before in history. Yet, in the United Kingdom, mathematics education is in crisis, and, with it, individual opportunities for development and the future economic prosperity of this country. We cannot recruit or retain the mathematics teachers we need, so that, already, large numbers of our pupils are in mathematics classes without a mathematically qualified teacher. We are creating a vicious circle, whereby a poor supply of mathematics teachers today ensures an even greater shortfall in the future: a shortfall not only in teacher supply but also in the abilities and understanding of a whole generation. It is not only the schools that are affected. The inadequate and uneven mathematics skills that first-year undergraduates bring to science, social science and technology degrees are something with which British universities have neither the resources nor the organization to cope. The quality of degrees in a wide range of key disciplines is under threat.

The importance of mathematics

Some academics and journalists argue that mathematics is over-admired and over-privileged in the planning of the school curriculum. Such views are consonant with the long-standing antipathy to mathematics and science of British (and especially Establishment British) life, and its domination first by classicists and later by lawyers and historians. Corelli Barnett (a historian himself) was shocked that in 1955 only one Permanent Secretary of a central government department had any scientific qualification. Yet, 40 years on, nothing had changed. In most of her cabinets Margaret Thatcher was the only scientist, and for the vast majority of Tony Blair's ministers, mathematics stopped with O level, or before.

This book argues that we pay far too little attention to mathematics; that our mathematics education is deeply inadequate and misconceived, and that we need, as a matter of urgency, to change not just current attitudes but also current practice. We need to rethink the nature of the mathematics curriculum for pupils in compulsory schooling; to change, and greatly increase, provision for older students and adult learners; and to improve the mis-match between school and university demands. Moreover, in all these areas, we need to refocus our attention on mathematics and not merely 'numeracy'.

Mathematics and 'numeracy'

As the distinction between mathematics and numeracy is one of the recurrent themes of the following chapters, it is worth clarifying from the start. The word 'numeracy' is not, outside educational circles, a commonly used or recognized term. (It does not even merit a place in the Microsoft Word spell-check dictionary, so that every time we type the word we are rewarded with a red warning line.) Government policy, however, is currently overwhelmingly concerned with numeracy in the sense of arithmetic and number sense. This preoccupation is apparent in primary schools (through the National Numeracy Strategy); post-16, where there is a major effort to promote the 'key skill' of 'application of number'; and in the new requirements for all beginning teachers, whatever their subject and level, to pass a basic arithmetic test. Indeed, there is a tendency in official documents to treat the two terms as synonymous: the National Numeracy Strategy (Department for Education and Employment, 1999) is subtitled 'Framework for teaching mathematics'.

But numeracy – in its current meaning of arithmetic and number sense – is not the same as mathematics. If we imply it is, or that only numeracy is needed by students, we do them, and our whole society, a grave disservice. Of course, the study of number must figure centrally in the development of children's mathematical thinking. However, mathematics goes far beyond number or 'numeracy'. This is not just because the learning of mathematics piles up more and more skills and techniques (although it does that too), but because it transforms people's ability to conceptualize and structure relationships, to model the world and to change it. As delegates at a recent conference on 'Mathematics for the New Millennium' explained, mathematics offers 'thinking tools'; encompasses 'all kinds of relations, all kinds of operations'; is the language in which the 'quantitative reasoning' of design work takes place; and develops the 'symbol sense' needed in a world where information technology (IT) is omnipresent, and where it both depends on, and itself transforms, mathematics (Hoyles, Morgan and Woodhouse, 1999: 64, 30, 43 and 27, respectively).

In arguing for the importance of mathematics education, and the urgency of reform, this book brings together a large body of research findings and statistical trends. These relate to the UK and the developed world as a whole, to processes of individual learning, to the determinants of wages and growth, and to the nature of mathematical thought. The authors are all established and well-known researchers; but this is the first time that a single volume has brought together the major conclusions of their work in mathematics education. In our view as editors, they offer a compelling case.

School mathematics today

This book appears at the time of a major reform of the National Curriculum for England and Wales and the launch of reformed A levels, reformed and renamed General National Vocational Qualifications (GNVQs), and reformed 'key skill' assessments. In the concluding pages of this chapter, we evaluate the likelihood that these changes will break the cycle of deficiencies in mathematics education that has operated throughout the twentieth century. First, however, we need to sketch in the context within which this cycle is perpetuated. Readers should note that the following paragraphs apply most fully to England. Wales and Northern

Ireland are broadly similar (but decreasingly so), and Scotland operates with quite different curriculum and testing arrangements.

The National Curriculum

The last two decades have seen a consistent movement towards ever-greater central control and 'accountability' in British education, which has moved from a state of unusual decentralization and freedom to innovate to having one of the most tightly controlled school systems in Europe. Since 1989 mathematics in state schools in England and Wales has been organized around the content and assessment methods of the National Curriculum: the independent sector is formally exempt, but in practice its teaching content is determined largely and increasingly by the same requirements. Teachers of mathematics of up to 11 years' experience have known only this centralized framework for teaching and for monitoring their pupils' progress.

For children, the National Curriculum represents a minimum entitlement and common progression routes until the age of 14. From 14 to 16, their school mathematics is determined by whichever General Certificate of Secondary Education (GCSE) course they are following, although GCSE syllabuses themselves must reflect the National Curriculum. For teachers, the National Curriculum requires that they structure their teaching around statutory content and national tests. Choices of teaching methods and resources rest with teachers, but are increasingly standardized via published materials which 'deliver' the National Curriculum via the National Numeracy Strategy. The latter is accompanied by non-statutory guidance on the structure of lessons, for grouping pupils within lessons and for teaching methods.

Accountability

Public accountability is secured (in theory) through a plethora of quangos and legislation, including the Office for Standards in Education (OFSTED). It inspects schools, teacher training institutions, local education authorities (LEAs) (in conjunction with the Audit Commission) and, soon, further education colleges. The Teacher Training Agency (TTA) exerts tight control over the content of teacher training courses (including, therefore, the preparation of both specialist and non-specialist teachers of mathematics). For the purposes of mathematics education, however, the most important accountability tool is the national assessment programme, which every year tests all seven, 11 and 14 year olds in state schools.

This programme is the responsibility of the Qualifications and Curriculum Authority (QCA), the quango with overall responsibility for the school curriculum (and thus the National Curriculum), and for all non-university-level qualifications delivered using public funding. The standardized National Curriculum tests (commonly known as Standardized Assessment Tasks or SATs) are only one among a plethora of publications, guidance, statutory orders and the like which emanate from the QCA, but they are also its most visible product. This is because test results are the basis for national league tables which rank schools in order of students' achievement in mathematics, English and science. They also provide teachers with a benchmark for their own assessments, and a clear signal about which parts of the National Curriculum are seen as most important.

GCSE examinations

The final two years of compulsory schooling (ages 14–16, years 10 and 11), as noted above, are dominated less by the National Curriculum as such than by the GCSE examinations. Taken typically at the end of compulsory schooling, GCSEs incorporate but also interpret and augment the basic curriculum, and allow for finer gradations of achievement than the broad 'levels' into which the National Curriculum is divided. The GCSE examinations, and their predecessors – O levels and Certificate of Secondary Education (CSE) – have played an enormous role in English, Welsh and Northern Irish education since the 1950s (as do their Scottish equivalents). They affect young people's chances on the labour market, their access to apprenticeship, their decisions about sixth-form study and their later university applications. While the UK is almost unique in having such high-profile, high-stakes public examinations at this age, there is little sign that governments, universities or employers have any desire to abandon them. Schools' GCSE results are given pride of place not only in league tables, but also in their own promotional literature and in OFSTED reports.

GCSE syllabuses provide courses of study at three different levels, or tiers, in response to the differentiated achievement levels among 14 year olds. (Consequently, the lower the tier, the further it falls short of the top National Curriculum level.) In addition, a small, but significant, proportion of 14–16 year olds study mathematics at levels below that of even the lowest GCSE tier. However, as Table 1.1 shows, the proportion of the age cohort obtaining a formal qualification in mathematics has risen steadily in recent years. It is impossible to know how much this reflects the National Curriculum reforms, and their guarantee of a minimum entitlement to all students in terms of curriculum provision, or how much it reflects the huge increase in staying on and qualification rates which has characterized this country, and indeed the whole developed world, in the last half-century.

Table 1.1 *Mathematics qualifications of year 11 (15–16-year-old) students, 1966–1998*

	No. of O levels GCEs/CSEs/GCSEs in mathematics attempted by year 11 candidates (000s)	As % year 11 population	Passes in mathematics as % year 11 population (all qualifications and pass grades combined)
1966 (England and Wales)	312	46	32
1972 (England and Wales)	449	64	48
1982 (England)	612	74	70
1992 (England)	461	81	76
1998 (England)	528	88	84

Note: CSE and GCE could both be taken by a given candidate and, therefore, results prior to GCSE may involve double counting.
Source: DES/DfEE Statistics of Education: School examinations (annual).

The differences in mathematical content and in assessment styles between the different GCSE courses are intended to ensure that all students are able to make progress, and are neither over nor under challenged. The tiers are designed to overlap so that, for example, it is possible to obtain a B grade through entry to either the top- or middle-tier examinations. However, this apparent parity masks real and significant differences in the nature of the mathematics studied and in the quality of the mathematical thinking required for success. These differences also have major implications for students' later opportunities and performance, a point to which later chapters (especially Chapters Four and Five) return in detail.

At GCSE level too, the last 20 years have meant increasing central control. Public examinations were developed, in the UK, not by government but by independent examination boards, the first of which were established by the universities to set matriculation exams for would-be undergraduates. Until recently, the boards were free to develop and examine their own syllabuses – subject only to these being popular enough with schools to be viable. This gave the school system considerable freedom to experiment, but also led to an enormous number of different syllabuses and examinations, not least in a large-entry subject such as mathematics.

Over the last two decades, however, the boards have in effect been nationalized and reduced increasingly to administrative arms of central government agencies. The rationale for this is the impossibility of monitoring (and, by extrapolation, maintaining) standards when there are so many different and only partially overlapping syllabuses. Boards have been reduced in number by a combination of central fiat and pressure to amalgamate, so that there are now only three large 'awarding bodies' offering GCSEs in England, and one each for the other countries of the UK. The QCA has been given major powers of oversight; GCSE examinations must all follow common criteria to keep them in line with the National Curriculum; and only a limited number of syllabuses and examinations in each subject are being approved for delivery in institutions receiving public funding.

Curriculum 2000
At the time of writing, the QCA has just completed a major review of the National Curriculum which, after consultation, will be implemented as Curriculum 2000. Under it, pupils in years 10 and 11 will follow one of two

statutory programmes in mathematics, either 'Foundation' or 'Higher' (QCA, July 1999), each underpinned by detailed and different programmes of study. Both the Foundation and the Higher programmes of study cover a wide range of mathematics. The Foundation programme is not confined to numeracy and the Higher programme specifies algebra, which should enable a smoother transition to A/S and A level courses, more geometry and trigonometry than at present, and more requirements for reasoning and proof to be taught and displayed. Programmes of study for the first year of secondary schooling have been published, as a sequel to the National Numeracy Strategy for primary schools.

These changes are a response to consistent criticisms of current provision, but have given rise to other concerns in their turn. The National Association of Mathematics Advisers is concerned about overload, especially for 11–14 year olds, warning that: 'At Key Stage 3 the programme of study is exceptionally detailed and specific, reflecting most of the level 7 requirements. Level 5 is the current expectation for the majority of pupils. We all know the perils of cramming too much too soon.'[1] More generally, it is clear that increased expectations for all students in compulsory schooling will only be realized if there are sufficient, appropriately qualified mathematics teachers. We return to this issue in the final part of this chapter.

The structure of the National Curriculum
It is a curious aspect of the National Curriculum that it was written without any prior systematic study of the rationale for the study of particular subjects or of how their content should relate to the requirements of higher education, industry, or general intellectual development. Instead, nominated subject committees battled their way to compromise, often with major upheavals *en route* (as when both the Chair and one member of the mathematics committee resigned amid major national publicity, or when the history committee divided into warring camps). At the same time, each area of the curriculum was subject to a common straitjacket in the form of requirements to adopt a given number of attainment levels and targets. In the case of mathematics, this originally involved ten levels for each of 14 separate attainment targets; later simplified into nine 'level

descriptions' (Levels 1–8 and a level of 'exceptional performance') across four broad areas of mathematics (attainment targets).

Fitting the possible content of the entire compulsory school curriculum into this framework of attainment targets and levels was what dominated the subject committees' endeavours. The original outcome – involving enough documents to sink a battleship and an assessment regime to match – created classroom havoc, especially at primary level, and has been subject to successive rewrites. These have reduced the load on teachers (in maths and elsewhere), while retaining the basic structure and compulsion of the curriculum.

Although the National Curriculum in mathematics has never been based on any systematic principles for deciding content or approach, this is not to say that its approach is arbitrary or inexplicable. On the contrary, one can identify two major sources of influence, one critical in the early days of the National Curriculum, the other of major recent and current importance. They are the Cockcroft Report on mathematics and, more recently, a series of comparative studies and international tests in which UK performance was compared with that of other countries.

The Cockcroft Report
The first version of the mathematics 'orders', which continue to define much of both the existing and the proposed post-2000 National Curriculum in mathematics, strongly reflects the philosophy of the 1982 Cockcroft Report – *Mathematics Counts, the Report of the Committee of Inquiry into the Teaching of Mathematics in Schools*. This committee was established in response to an urgent recommendation to that effect by the 1977 Parliamentary Expenditure Committee, which noted that:

> there is a large number of questions about the mathematical attainments of children which need much more careful analysis than we have been able to give. ... These concern the apparent lack of basic computational skills in many children, the increasing mathematical demands made on adults, the lack of qualified maths teachers ... the lack of communication between further and higher education, employers and schools about each group's needs and view points.

Over 20 years later, almost all these concerns have become more, not less, pressing, as the following chapters show.

The Cockcroft Report made a large number of recommendations and, although not all were implemented, in key respects it set the tone for mathematics education over the next 15 years. Of particular importance were its emphases on practical and 'real-life' applications, which fed into the National Curriculum's strong early emphasis on using and applying mathematics. It argued in paragraph 451: 'We believe it should be a fundamental principle that no topic should be included unless it can be developed sufficiently for it to be applied in ways which the pupils can understand.' This sounds completely unexceptional, and indeed was generally seen as such at the time. However, as some critics pointed out then (Goldstein and Wolf, 1983), and as Chapter Six in this volume makes abundantly clear, moving from general precept to practical implementation is far from simple. It is by no means self-evident what is 'understandable' and an appropriate application for a particular class or student. The Cockcroft team seem to have envisaged a straightforward packaging of mathematics in contexts of 'everyday use'. Yet one person's motivating and relevant context is another's crashing bore. Charts of waterways may seem a wonderful context for maths teaching to a keen sailor, and completely irrelevant to a group of 16 year olds interested in computer gaming or clubbing (but rarely both). Mortgage payments may motivate a banker, but hardly the average year 10 class. How many of these find shopping list and supermarket questions wildly more interesting than those mythological diggers of ditches?

In general, the Cockcroft Report presents mathematics as very much a series of skills (for which different free-standing applications can then be devised). This concept imbues its strong recommendation that mathematics teaching be organized around a 'foundation list' of topics which every student could fully master. The influence of the Committee's thinking is also evident directly and indirectly throughout the mathematics National Curriculum. The latter presents the curriculum as a list of separate skills (very similar to Cockcroft's 'foundation list'); while the pre-2000 version's downgrading of algebra and virtual exclusion of any teaching of proof or formal geometry reflect not merely the drafters' own views but also common post-Cockcroft practice in English schools. (For extended discussions of this issue, see Dowling and Noss, 1990; London Mathematical Society, 1995; Hoyles, 1997; Hoyles and Healy, 1999; Royal Society, 1997.) The Cockcroft message was that the range of school mathematics for the vast majority can and, indeed, should be highly limited; and while its most visible and immediate impact on the National Curriculum was in the latter's strong early emphasis on 'applications', its most consistent and longer-lasting impact was through its advocacy of a limited diet of numeracy for most students and most adults.

This view was bolstered by the Cockcroft report's interpretation of the mathematics needed in adult life: namely extremely limited and reductionist. 'It is of fundamental importance to appreciate ... that all the mathematics which is used at work is related directly to specific and often limited tasks which soon become familiar', it opined in paragraph 83. Then in paragraph 85: 'We believe that it is possible to summarize a very large part of the mathematical needs of employment as "a feeling for measurement".'

This book demonstrates how profoundly misconceived this was as a recipe for a modern economy, but it is not merely a monument to the perils of predicting even the next 20 years. It was also the result of the way the committee and its researchers approached the topic. Their practice was to look at a workplace and identify any particular identifiable techniques – whether addition or integration – which happened to be visible and routinely applied. In our view, this is profoundly to misunderstand the way in which people think mathematically. It also assumes a world in which the design of a workplace is the responsibility of a small élite, with everyone else being allocated a pre-defined and limited task for which they can be trained. This is not only inegalitarian, but a recipe for economic stagnation.

International comparisons

The current tendency to emphasize 'numeracy' at the expense of mathematics received its strongest impetus from a series of international tests and comparisons and their impact on politicians. Successive studies have tended to show British children performing far worse than others on basic arithmetic items: among them a series of detailed studies carried out by the National Institute of Economic and Social Research (NIESR) and, later, the University of Exeter, comparing English schools and vocational education programmes with those of Germany, the Netherlands and Switzerland. These studies often included a comparison of the perform-ance of small groups of young people on items such as fraction and decimal operations (in which English performance was invariably worse) and received wide press coverage (Jaworski and Phillips, 1999).

The most influential findings have been those from large international surveys, notably the Third International Mathematics and Science Study (TIMSS), organized by the International Association for the Evaluation of Educational Achievement (IEA), which compared the performance of students in a large number of countries. The results of the maths tests in particular were very widely reported, and showed English children perform-ing far less well than those of the Pacific Rim in particular, and than some major European countries, *especially on basic arithmetic and number items*. (In science, the English students did extremely well.) The Inter-national Adult Literacy Survey similarly showed English respondents performing relatively poorly. These findings helped to create an environ-ment in which many politicians apparently believed that no English child could do any arithmetic at all. Complaints from businessmen about the educational standards of school-leavers similarly found (and find) a regular place in both broadsheet and tabloid newspapers. The result has been an increasing emphasis on basic number skills and a tendency to regard these as the most, or even the only, important part of mathematics.

Mathematics in post-compulsory education
Up to now, we have been describing the mathematics curriculum of the compulsory school. Although highly distinctive in some ways, at this level the UK is generally very much in line with the developed world as a whole, all of whose countries recommend or prescribe a wide general education for all young people (Green, Wolf and Leney, 1999). After age

16, however, the UK diverges dramatically from the general pattern. Chapter Five discusses this divergence and its consequences in some detail. Here we will sketch in the basic outline of mathematics provision in upper secondary education.

Since the 1950s, the English (and the Welsh and Northern Irish) 'sixth form', covering the final two years of secondary education, has been distinguished by its extreme specialization. Having obtained a variety of public certificates in a range of subjects at age 16, the typical academic track student then proceeds to study three, or sometimes four, subjects only at advanced – 'A' – level. This set of A levels may or may not include mathematics, but for a very high proportion of this group, who are generally university-bound, it will not. Nine per cent of the age cohort and 25 per cent of A level candidates at most include a mathematics A or AS level in their studies. It is worth noting that the Cockcroft Report, to which we have referred above, made a number of small suggestions for reforms in sixth-form mathematics, but no major recommendations for change in either content or the numbers/proportions taking mathematics. Indeed, the proportion of space the report allocates to sixth-form mathematics is very small.

A level students are by far the largest single group of sixth formers, and now include well over one-third of the age cohort. In addition, a large number of students stay in full-time education following vocational or quasi-vocational courses such as GNVQs or Business and Technician Education Council (BTEC) diplomas. These awards, like A levels, offer the opportunity to proceed to higher education. Other students take specific vocational training or enter apprenticeships. Of this non-A level group, a small number will receive dedicated maths tuition (notably those in engineering or science programmes); most will not. Others will receive yet more 'numeracy' lessons in preparation for the 'key skills' test in application of number which originally formed a compulsory part of GNVQs and is now being offered as part of a free-standing 'key skills' qualification. Many will also re-take their maths GCSE in pursuit of the magic C grade which most universities and employers want (and which is often a prerequisite for entry into an A level programme). This book (and especially Chapters Three, Four and Five) will argue that this limited range of provision is hugely and increasingly inadequate.

Few people, and certainly none of this book's authors, would deny the importance of numeracy, and of ensuring that children obtain a secure grasp of arithmetic and a 'feeling' for number. However, current government policy is so weighted towards number skills and towards encouraging and funding the repeated testing of basic arithmetic, as to indicate a belief that this is all the majority of people, and the bulk of a modern economy, needs. The following chapters show, from a variety of perspectives, how wrong this is, and how urgently change is needed.

Teacher supply

Important though it may be, it is not enough simply to convince policy-makers of the need for more extensive and better mathematics education. Students do not teach themselves: and while some enthusiasts have convinced themselves that information and communications technology (ICT) will create the teacher-proof and teacherless classroom, there is no evidence whatsoever to support them. Even the expensive and highly promoted systems which provide diagnosis, drill and feedback in basic arithmetic turn out, on careful evaluation, to produce little or no significant improvement in children's performance (Wood, 1998). So we are back to teachers.

Worries over teacher supply are nothing new. We noted earlier that, in 1977, Parliament was expressing its strong concern over the lack of qualified mathematics teachers. Since then, unfortunately, things have moved from bad to worse. The remainder of this chapter addresses the state of mathematics teacher recruitment today, and the implications for mathematics education's future.

The current shortfall

If the next generation of young people is to be taught mathematics effectively, then we need to produce enough aspiring teachers and keep them in the classroom. The prognosis is gloomy. As we discuss further in the text, despite the implementation of the National Curriculum, from the mid 1980s the numbers of post-16 students who choose to study mathematics has declined in absolute terms and stagnated in relative terms; while the numbers and proportions of 15 year olds following the more advanced GCSE courses has plummeted. Higher Education Statistics Agency (HESA) figures reveal that the proportion of those graduating in mathematical sciences, as a proportion of all graduates, has fallen steeply since the mid 1980s. University Grants Committee figures for 1987 indicate that mathematics degrees amounted to more than five per cent of the total degrees awarded that year, while the HESA figures for 1995–1998, given in Table 1.2, show the current proportion to be well under two per cent. Although absolute numbers of graduates are fairly steady (reflecting the huge increase in student numbers), the demand and expanding opportunities for mathematics graduates are reflected in the falling numbers attracted by teaching. If we consider undergraduate numbers in conjunction with figures for the numbers and proportions proceeding to PGCE courses and with the Department for Education and Employment (DfEE) target figures for mathematics initial teacher training (ITT), the actual and prospective shortfalls in supply become obvious.

Table 1.2 *Numbers graduating in mathematical sciences after full-time or part-time study in England and Wales, compared with graduates in all subjects. Numbers proceeding to PGCE courses as compared with the ITT target figures*

Year	A Number of mathematics graduates	B Total number of graduates	C Column A as % of column B	D Number of maths graduates proceeding to PGCE	E Column D as % of column A	F DfEE target for maths ITT recruitment
1995	3,540	192,260	1.8	514	14.5	unknown
1996	3,537	201,390	1.8	421	11.9	2,700
1997	3,296	203,226	1.6	398	12.1	2,370
1998	3,717	202,204	1.8	308	8.3	2,270

Source: Teacher Training Agency: Annual Reports; Higher Education Statistics Agency: First destinations of students leaving higher education institutions (annual).

The DfEE sets targets for recruitment in each subject each year. The likelihood of meeting those will depend partly on the numbers of those on undergraduate courses at the present time and also on the attractions of teaching. Between 1995 and 1999 the numbers of mathematics graduates proceeding to a PGCE course fell by 40 per cent. An adequate supply of fully qualified mathematics teachers will depend to a large extent on reversing this trend.

Teacher supply requirements are now modelled (Department for Education and Employment, 1998a) in order to set targets for ITT. These targets are then used by the TTA in planning and funding training courses. The Secondary Teacher Supply Model accommodates several factors affecting the numbers of mathematics teachers required, including distributions of pupils of different ages, curriculum changes, the perceived amount of teaching time to be allocated to mathematics, and inflow and outflow of teachers prior to retirement age. (Not all successful ITT completers go on to teach in primary or secondary schools after obtaining a PGCE. Overall, around 10 per cent each year do not enter teaching, but in mathematics recent drop-out rates are twice this level (Higher Education Statistical Agency, 1996–1998; Hansard, 2000).) The DfEE also sees the need for a recruitment factor in order to redress the 'imbalance between teachers' qualifications and subjects taught' – a piece of careful civil servants' prose to which we return below (Department for Education and Employment, 1998a).

Comparing the HESA figures for new mathematics graduates with the targets for mathematics ITT shows that, if mathematics teachers were all to be drawn from recent mathematics graduates, *more than half of the new graduates would have to register for ITT*. In fact, of course, nothing of the sort occurs. Instead, a great deal of recruitment is from other sources, including older entrants and graduates in other, mathematically related, disciplines. Even so, and not surprisingly, recruitment has been and remains highly problematic. Actual recruitment for 1998–1999, for example, was 48 per cent below target (Teacher Training Agency, 1999). In 1999–2000 'golden handshake' incentives offered a £5,000 grant (discussed further below) in shortage subjects, including mathematics. This had a one-off effect: the TTA was able to report that both applications and acceptances were up by over 30 per cent as compared with 1998. Even so, this left numbers well below target figures for a few years back and the impact was not sustained. In spring 2000, with mathematics recruitment targets up, actual recruitment was way down – 20 per cent down on the same period in 1999, and at a level which was well under half that of 1995. The government's panicked response – a training salary for all PGCE students, which is higher for shortage subjects – should increase recruitment, but may or may not increase the numbers actually entering the classroom. Meanwhile, staff turnover is rising: in 1998 the number leaving state school teaching was 50 per cent up on five years earlier. If recruitment is healthy, this need not matter: in shortage subjects, it compounds the problem.

Recruitment figures are only part of the story (not only because of turnover, but also because they reflect what the TTA sees as critical and possible, rather than what it might like to achieve). Unfilled posts are another indication of supply problems, but also greatly underestimate the scale of the problem. The DfEE recorded 141 unfilled mathematics posts in secondary schools in 1998, and as each teacher of mathematics will be responsible for around 150 pupils on a conservative estimate, this implies that at least 20,000 children in England and Wales lacked a qualified mathematics teacher in that year. However, this figure conceals the true situation, because it does not record the extent to which posts were filled, and mathematics teaching carried out – but by teachers whose higher education was in other disciplines.

Profiles of practising and trainee teachers
A secondary mathematics teacher should have a degree involving a considerable proportion of mathematics, whether this be a BEd degree, a maths degree, or another degree (e.g. engineering) with high maths content. The highest levels of formal mathematics qualifications of teachers of mathematics are recorded annually by the DfEE in 'Statistics of Education: Teachers' from data collected in the 'Secondary Schools Curriculum and Staffing Survey'. In 1996–1997, for example, 40 per cent of those teaching secondary mathematics (years 7–13) had a degree in mathematics (pure,

applied or statistics), and a further 40 per cent were qualified in mathematics beyond A level standard predominantly through BEd degrees, PGCE certificates and Certificates in Education (a qualification last awarded in the early 1970s) in which mathematics would have been a main subject. However, no fewer than 20 per cent were recorded with 'no qualification' in mathematics; their teaching qualification was in another subject, and they may or may not have had an A level in mathematics.

These teachers numbered approximately 5,000 of the total number of approximately 25,000 teachers of some mathematics in that year. Elsewhere in the statistics it emerges that this last group provided only nine per cent of tuition in mathematics overall, and were more likely to be teaching younger pupils (11 per cent of tuition in years 7–9, eight per cent of tuition in years 10–11 and three per cent of tuition in years 12–13). This is an obvious way for schools to adapt to a supply crisis. Nonetheless, younger (and also less able) pupils are as entitled as their peers – by the National Curriculum as well as by natural justice – to teaching which offers the full range of mathematical experiences in the curriculum. That means they need teachers with a broad and rigorous base of mathematical knowledge as well as knowledge of how to teach mathematics.

Current figures underline the parlous state of current provision, and also how ill-equipped we are to expand the teaching and learning of mathematics, as we need to. Nor can one even use TTA targets – themselves reduced from a few years ago – as a measure of future provision. Fully qualified mathematics teachers are also by no means all destined for the state schools or even the school sector as a whole (as implied by the ITT targeting process). DfEE statistics (1998b) show that between 1995 and 1997 around 70 per cent of fully qualified mathematics teachers were employed in state schools. The remaining 30 per cent were teaching in independent schools or in the further education sector.

The shortage of young mathematicians entering teaching means that higher education must recruit mathematics teachers from sources other than final-year undergraduates. And indeed we do. Beginning maths teachers are recruited from a range of disciplines, at a wide variety of ages, many of them coming to teaching after experience in other fields.

Until the mid 1970s, the acceptable degrees for secondary mathematics teachers were 'mathematics' or 'mathematics with physics'. Combined degrees in two or three subjects, including mathematics, then became acceptable. Today, the range of acceptable degrees has broadened further still. In our own institution, we look for a minimum of 50 per cent mathematical content in the applicant's degree: or, in cases where degree content is borderline, for good mathematics A level results or a higher degree in a numerate discipline. Other institutions will have different criteria, but a general result of the change is the need to build subject knowledge into PGCE courses alongside all the other burgeoning requirements.

As a nation we also, to a striking degree, depend on the graduates of other countries' systems. Table 1.3 summarizes the characteristics of two

Table 1.3 *Profile of mathematics PGCE students – Institute of Education, London*

	Class of Degree*	% of degrees with maths as named subject	Education overseas: secondary (%)	Education overseas: degree (%)	Mean age	Age at start of course	% in teaching posts in autumn term after QTS
1998–1999 n = 43 (F: 20 M: 23)	1: 1 2.1: 9 2.2: 19 3: 5 Pass: 9	70	23	16	27.7 years (range = 20 years)	20–24:16 25–29:12 30–34: 9 35–39: 5 40–44: 1	74%
1999–2000 n = 42 (F: 18 M: 24)	1: 8 2.1: 14 2.2: 12 3: 4 Pass: 3 MSc: 1	62	29	10	29.9 years (range = 30 years)	20–24:18 25–29: 9 30–34: 3 35–39: 5 40–44: 3 45–49: 0 50–54: 4	76%

Note: *This is the class of the degree which qualified the applicant for a place on the course. In some cases the applicant also has a higher degree.
Source: Unpublished data, Mathematical Sciences Group, Institute of Education.

successive groups of mathematics Postgraduate Certificate of Education (PGCE) students, again in our own institution. These figures cannot be extrapolated to the national scene, as institutions vary in their catchment area and profile. Nonetheless, the average age of our students underlines the extent to which we draw on entrants other than new maths graduates: and the figures on numbers educated overseas demonstrate how much we rely on other countries to supply mathematics teachers for our children.

Recruitment incentives

Common sense and econometric models agree that pay has a powerful influence on teacher recruitment and retention; and this has particularly affected mathematics teaching. Mathematics qualifications have high market value, as Chapter Three makes clear. The pressing need to select, recruit and retain high-quality teachers is recognized in the Green Paper, *Teachers Meeting the Challenge of Change* (Department for Education and Employment, 1998c). It proposed several measures to increase recruitment in shortage subjects such as mathematics, including the 'golden handshake' mentioned earlier – a £2,500 award to all students who registered on PGCE courses followed by another £2,500 when they were appointed as newly qualified teachers (Teacher Training Agency, 1999).

More diverse routes towards qualified teacher status (QTS) are also being developed to make entry easier, notably the provision of school-based training places in mathematics where students are paid as assistant teachers and receive education in school towards the common QTS standards. The consortia of schools which currently provide school-based teacher training are also to be increased in number. However, although ready access to QTS and financial rewards are obviously very important, teaching is hardly likely ever to be a profession in which the prime attraction is salary. If we are to recruit good teachers – and we should be looking for many *more* maths teachers in the future, to teach more maths, better, for longer and to more students – then we also need to consider intrinsic rewards. Therefore, we finish with a brief look at how new teachers currently feel about their work.

Perceptions of practising teachers

The briefest glance at the education press makes it clear that many teachers feel angry and disillusioned. They complain that they are constantly criticized, inundated with directives and requirements, and that their professionalism is being undermined. This is hardly a picture guaranteed to boost recruitment. However, it is always difficult to know how far either vocal individuals or official representatives of the profession actually reflect classroom teachers' views. Therefore, we have used our own ex-students, at the Institute of Education, to provide a different perspective on those who become maths teachers and why; and how likely they are to stay. While we clearly cannot generalize for the country as a whole, nonetheless their individual histories and voices are indicative of the teaching force we are creating and will depend on in the next few decades.

During interviews for PGCE courses many applicants reveal that they have had a long-term aim to become a mathematics teacher. They often express admiration for one or more of their own past teachers, but sometimes they have been motivated by poor experiences of learning mathematics in school, either on their own behalf or in sympathy with a sibling or close friend. Other applicants have become motivated to teach after following another career path for some years. They perceive mathematics teaching as challenging, worthwhile and interesting in comparison with office-based jobs in finance or industry. Some look forward to school mathematics itself, to their professional responsibilities to pass on their knowledge and understanding to their pupils, and to motivating children by presenting mathematics in an interesting way.

The following extract from recently recorded discussions between practising teachers who were recent graduates illustrates how they balance their statutory requirements with their aims for their pupils' mathematical understanding:

> Interviewer: How have the reforms affected your actual work as teachers; first of all the National Curriculum and SATs and now the target-setting? It's sounding to me as though you see them having a positive effect.

Teacher A: Personally, I think it is positive because it allows you to focus on what you need to achieve and if you've been teaching a child from year 7 onwards you know what grades he's likely to achieve. It all depends on his motivation, how much he understands maths and how much he enjoys it. There are some who are just very difficult to motivate and you can see that they are going down.

Teacher B: There's a lot of build-up before the SATs. We build the kids up because obviously we want them to try to do the best they can, even in paper 1 without calculators. They are set in our school for maths and they only compare themselves with those in their class. So if everyone in their class got level 3 or 4, I'd say to them that they'd just missed the target. They don't necessarily know how far they missed it by ... or you have a higher set where they all get maybe a 5 or 6 and they don't mind too much just being one level away from each other. Well that's what comes across. I can't see it puts great pressure on the children.

Among our students, there were many with personal difficulties, with implications not only for recruitment but also long-term retention within mathematics teaching. An end-of-course questionnaire (1997–1998) revealed those as predominantly financial, with six receiving support through the Institute's hardship fund. Other difficulties included access to ICT for those with no computer at home and with relatively limited background in using a computer – an issue of considerable importance given the growing importance of ICT in the curriculum and especially in mathematics teaching.

Therefore, it is gratifying (as well as critical for English mathematics education) that so many of these students do surmount the inherent difficulties in the course, gain QTS and enter teaching. As Table 1.3 shows, three-quarters of the 1998 intake have been working as mathematics teachers since September 1999, all in state schools. Whether or not they continue as mathematics teachers will depend in most cases on their experiences and levels of job satisfaction during their first few years in schools. Discussions with practising teachers give some insight into their attitudes – and the likelihood that they will remain.

Teacher C: There's a lot of competition for maths graduates in other types of employment, so they've got a bigger choice. Teaching isn't necessarily seen as a highly rewarding profession either financially or in other ways.

Interviewer: Do you have friends who did your degree courses at the same time who are doing something else ?

Teacher C: I haven't really kept in touch but I know that at the end of my degree there were only two of us who were thinking of going into teaching and then I left it for five years and went into ...

Interviewer: And remind me why you came back to the idea of teaching

Teacher C: It was something that in the back of my mind I had wanted to do for an awfully long time. I was 45 and if I didn't do it then it was going to be too late. So I tried it and have no real regrets except that some days I wonder what I'm doing.

Teacher B: You're in there and you're teaching someone and you think, 'I'm enjoying this.' You can't actually see many outcomes. Whereas when you're at work you're in a nicer environment. When you're a teacher and you're in front of the class you can't go off to the loo or have your coffee when you want. You're not going to be sent away for business meetings or have lunch in the pub and talk to adults all the time. Teaching doesn't look glamorous and you can't put across to people what it's like to actually sit there and help those children – I don't know how to put across to others how enjoyable this is.

Teacher C: I have to say that in my case anyway there are more frustrations than there are successes. Every so often you see a kid progressing and you think, 'That's great.' But one of the things I came to terms with early on is that teaching isn't a job you're ever going to reach perfection in. You've just got to keep aiming for that and do as well as you can.

Teacher A: The government is pushing for performance-related pay, talking about salaries of about £35,000 for some teachers.

Interviewer: Any indication of how many teachers that would be ?

Teacher B: I think they need to make us all super teachers and not have a differentiated sort of thing. It certainly implies that you're either a super teacher or you're no good – just there to fill the space.

Teachers' comments underscore the importance of factors other than pay in attracting them to the profession and keeping them there. These are also the factors that can drive them away. A recent study of London teachers who were quitting the profession showed that, for many, flexibility and more room for creativity and initiative were just as important as pay (TTA, 1999). We need to attract thousands more mathematics teachers, urgently: to maintain current school provision, but also, as this book argues, to expand it substantially, especially for our older students. Without major changes in pay and conditions and career options, this seems all too unlikely.

Conclusion

The world of the new millennium, and of the twenty-first century, is one of constant technological change, globalization, and an IT-based communications revolution. These points have become banal but are no less true for all that. In this world, we will argue, mathematics is fundamental as never before: and our education must recognize this.

In some respects, the government is coming to perceive the need for change. The dire effect on people's lives of very low basic skills, described in Chapter Two, is increasingly recognized. It is a major force behind the national numeracy strategy, the razzmatazz of 'Maths Year 2000', and the introduction of compulsory mathematics tests for trainee teachers. The Skills Taskforce, headed by the chief executive of the British Chambers of Commerce, has called for a greatly expanded role for mathematics among young people and adults, in education and training; and QCA has developed and launched Free-Standing Mathematics Units: new mini-qualifications for sixth formers not taking AS or A level mathematics – which is to say the vast majority.

But small reforms and spin-doctoring are, in the end, just that. Vast effort is going into promoting 'Key Skills' across the curriculum for all 16–19 year olds. This largely involves dressing up work from other subjects as a 'Key Skills' in number, IT and communication qualification. It may look good in league tables and press releases; but it will do absolutely nothing substantive to turn the country's young people into a mathematically literate generation. Nor will a Maths Year 2000 advertising extravaganza which plugs the importance of mathematics by showing parents counting their children's press-ups.

This lack of vision no doubt reflects our historical failure to take mathematics – or science – seriously, and the persistence of a society which encourages its élite to abandon, and often belittle, mathematics from an early age. But the result is to deprive our children of opportunity and choice, and to stunt them not simply as future entrepreneurs and employees, but also as citizens and human beings.

The reality is that we start the new century with shrinking mathematics provision and an ongoing crisis in mathematics teacher recruitment which threatens the quality even of what we offer now. Will the mathematics classrooms of the twenty-first century be nonetheless stimulating and rewarding places to work? And will they provide the country, and its citizens, with the skills and creativity they need? This book will, we hope, convince readers that this can happen only with major reforms – and that such reforms are possible, necessary and long overdue.

Notes

1. Quoted in 'Developing the School Curriculum', QCA, August 1999.

2 The Impact of Poor Numeracy on Employment and Career Progression

John Bynner and Samantha Parsons
Centre for Longitudinal Studies, Institute of Education, University of London

Introduction

Literacy is a basic skill which few people in a modern industrial society can afford to be without but, until recently, the importance of numeracy in employment has been less recognized. Yet poor numeracy skills are a major disadvantage for adults, particularly in the ever more demanding world of work. Surveys have shown that both men and women lacking numeracy skills are more likely in their early careers to be out of the labour market, or engaged in low-grade work in unskilled manual jobs without training (Ekinsmyth and Bynner, 1994; Bynner and Parsons, 1997a; Carey, Low and Hansboro, 1997; Parsons and Bynner, 1999).

Perhaps more importantly, the demand for numeracy and mathematics skills in the modern labour market is remarkably high and is increasing. In a study carried out by the Institute for Manpower Studies in 1992, it was concluded that only one in eight jobs did not require any numeracy skills at all and only one in four had minimal numeracy requirements, i.e. skills at the Basic Skills Agency 'Foundation level' (Atkinson and Spilsbury, 1993; Atkinson, Spilsbury and Williams, 1993). The increasing demand for numeracy skills is particularly apparent in selling jobs and semi-skilled manual jobs. Besides jobs requiring specific computational and measurement skills in the building trades, engineering and sales, a wide range of occupations, especially in offices, depend increasingly on the use of information technology (IT), where some basic understanding of the logic of IT applications can increase efficiency. Demands for more financial accountability at all levels of employment also confront increasing numbers of employees with the need for competence in accounting and computational skills.

The question arises from these employment trends as to what impact they are having on the individual worker. We need to know the relative effects of literacy difficulties and numeracy difficulties on employment problems: whether literacy is the fundamental problem which overrides any effects of poor numeracy, or whether numeracy represents a signifi-cant problem in its own right.[1] This chapter attempts to answer this question and others concerning basic numeracy: later chapters discuss more advanced mathematics. We start by examining evidence on the impact of early circumstances and experience on the acquisition of numeracy skills. We then turn to the relationship between poor numeracy and performance in the labour market. Finally we examine the decline of numeracy skills with time out of employment, and provide some policy implications to conclude the chapter.

The data

Our evidence comes from analysis of data on basic skills, collected in two of Britain's birth cohort studies. These are national longitudinal enquiries, based on following up single samples of people from birth into adulthood. The National Child Development Study (NCDS) has collected data on over 17,000 people born in a single week in 1958, and subse-quently at ages seven, 11, 16, 23, 33 and 37 (ten per cent sample). The 1970 British Cohort Study (BCS70) similarly began with a sample of over 17,000 people born in a single week in 1970, who have been followed up in subsequent surveys at ages five, ten, 16, 21 (ten per cent sample) and most recently at 26. At earlier ages information was collected using a variety of sources including interviews with parents, teachers and medical professionals, educational tests and self-completion questionnaires. In adult life cohort members gave information about their employment, family life and health, attitudes and citizenship. In both studies the cohort members in the ten per cent sample interview also sat functional literacy and numeracy assessments. Functional literacy and numeracy as defined by the Basic Skills Agency (BSA) is 'the ability to read, write and speak in English and use mathematics at a level necessary to function and progress at work and in society in general'. These assessment scores have formed the basis of a series of studies using birth cohort data carried out for the Adult Literacy and Basic Skills Unit (ALBSU) and more recently the Basic Skills Unit; (BSA) (ALBSU, 1987; Ekinsmyth and Bynner, 1994; Bynner and Steedman, 1995; Bynner and Parsons, 1997a; Bynner, Morphy and Parsons, 1997; Parsons and Bynner, 1998).

Assessment of numeracy and literacy
The assessments for BCS70 cohort members were devised by consultants, Cambridge Training and Development Ltd, and for NCDS cohort members by the National Foundation for Educational Research. Each test comprised much the same kinds of questions based around a visual stimulus that cohort members were likely to come across in their everyday lives, such as calculating change in a shop. BCS70 cohort members had ten numeracy and nine literacy tasks. NCDS cohort members had nine numeracy and eight literacy tasks. Each task had two or three sub-questions. They were administered to respondents at the end of a 45-minute interview, and on average took about half an hour to complete. The tasks were designed to tap skills at each of the different levels corresponding to the BSA 'Number Power' and 'Word Power' standards. For numeracy these are Foundation, Level 1 and Level 2; and for literacy they are Foundation, Level 1, Level 2 and Level 3. Foundation level, which is our principal focus here, represents a minimum level of skill, below which anybody is unlikely to be able to function effectively in the workplace. Table 2.1 gives examples of the kinds of numeracy performance standard set at each level by the BSA in the four designated areas: handling cash; keeping numerical or graphical records; planning the use of time or money; and calculating lengths, volumes and areas.[2] Table 2.2 gives an example of the questions answered by the NCDS cohort members at each numeracy level, together with the overall percentage who failed to answer correctly.

Table 2.1 *Simplified assessment scheme for numeracy skills*

Numeracy skill 1 Handle cash or other financial transaction accurately, using till, calculator or ready reckoner as necessary	*Foundation Level* Transactions of up to seven similar items at a time, give change if necessary	*Level 1* Transactions of up to 20 items at a time, give change and calculate simple discounts	*Level 2* Transactions of any number of items at a time, and calculate complex discounts, *or* use foreign currency
Numeracy skill 2 Keep records in numerical or graphical form	*Foundation Level* Record simple numerical information (e.g. count small batches)	*Level 1* Find the appropriate information and make a simple record based on it (e.g. simple stock-taking)	*Level 2* Find the appropriate information from several complex sources, make a record based on it (e.g. stock-taking and sales audit
Numeracy skill 3 Make and monitor schedules or budgets in order to plan the use of time or money	*Foundation Level* Plan and monitor small amounts of time and money (up to seven days or £250)	*Level 1* Plan and monitor amounts of time, money or expenditure (up to four weeks or £2,000)	*Level 2* Plan and monitor large amounts of time, money or spending (over four weeks or up to £20,000)
Numeracy skill 4 Calculate lengths, areas, weights or volumes accurately using appropriate tools (e.g. rulers and calculators)	*Foundation Level* Simple calculations on familiar items in either metric or imperial units	*Level 1* Calculations on items of unfamiliar or irregular shape in either metric or imperial units	*Level 2* Calculations on items of complex or composite shape, use scale drawings, convert between metric and imperial units

Source: Basic Skills Agency.

Table 2.2 *Examples of numeracy questions and the percentage who answered numeracy tasks* incorrectly

Questions	All % incorrect	Men % incorrect	Women % incorrect
Foundation level			
Cohort members were shown a train timetable and details of a job interview they were going to attend. Their task was to plan a route for a job interview.			
(a) Which train should you catch to arrive at company in time?	21	22	20
(b) What time will you arrive at the company?	34	33	35
Level 1			
Cohort members were going to spend the evening watching videos with a group of friends. There were six of them in total. They decided to order a pizza. The cost of a video and the pizza was given.			
(a) What is the total cost?	11	10	13
(b) How much does each person have to pay?	17	16	19
Level 2			
Cohort members were buying a new suite of furniture on credit. They were shown loan rates from a bank and from a hire purchase company. They had to decide the following.			
(a) Which is the cheapest way of paying monthly?	16	14	18
(b) Which is the cheapest way of paying overall?	18	16	20
(c) And by how much cheaper is it overall?	39	34	43
	n = 1,702	799	903

Source: NCDS.

Prevalence of numeracy and literacy difficulties

From an examination of significant cut-off points in the distribution of total scores on these tests a 'very low' scoring group could be identified

(Ekinsmyth and Bynner, 1994; Bynner and Parsons, 1997a). In the younger BCS70 cohort, 18 per cent of cohort members were assessed with a poor grasp of numeracy, and six per cent were assessed as having a poor grasp of literacy. Comparable figures for the older NCDS cohort were 23 per cent and six per cent. These cohort members were performing at or below Foundation Level. An additional 13 per cent of the NCDS cohort were identified with barely functional literacy skills, at or below Level 1 (defined as 'low'). Most of the analysis reported here is based on the NCDS data.

Early signs of poor adult numeracy

Adults with poor numeracy struggled at the first stages of formal education. At the ages seven, 11 and 16 the cohort members were given mathematics and reading tests in school.[3] Maths test scores at the early ages correctly predicted the people who later on would have the poorest numeracy scores as adults. Table 2.3 gives the mean (average) maths test scores (rescaled to 0–10) at ages seven, 11 and 16 for the NCDS cohort by the four numeracy groups at age 37.

The predictive power of the tests in identifying adult numeracy problems was less evident in the monitoring of children's skill development by teachers. Figure 2.1 shows that although teachers were able to identify 60 per cent of the people in the 'very low' numeracy groups as 'slow learners' when they were at primary school, they had only limited success in spotting those whose maths skills were very poor (nine per cent had 'little ability') at the age of seven.

Early influences on poor adult skills

An analysis of the characteristics associated with poor adult basic skills suggests that disadvantaged home circumstances, coupled with lack of parental interest and involvement in their children's education, constitute a bigger threat to the development of numeracy skills than literacy skills (Bynner and Steedman, 1995; Parsons and Bynner, 1998).

Table 2.3 *Mean scores attained in maths tests at seven, 11 and 16 by numeracy at 37*

Numeracy scores at 37	**Mathematics tests**								
	Age 7			Age 11			Age 16		
	Mean	sd	*N*	Mean	sd	*N*	Mean	sd	*N*
Men									
Very low	4.0	2.4	*128*	2.1	1.8	*120*	2.7	1.7	*108*
Low	4.8	2.1	*163*	3.5	2.1	*153*	3.7	1.7	*126*
Average	5.6	2.3	*175*	4.5	2.2	*174*	4.9	2.0	*144*
Good	6.6	2.3	*241*	6.2	2.2	*238*	6.3	2.0	*220*
Women									
Very low	4.1	2.3	*206*	2.3	1.7	*200*	2.5	1.4	*177*
Low	4.9	2.2	*224*	4.0	1.9	*212*	3.8	1.6	*188*
Average	5.9	2.3	*201*	5.1	2.2	*195*	4.9	2.0	*170*
Good	6.4	2.2	*172*	6.5	2.0	*160*	6.1	2.1	*145*
Max score	**10**			**10**			**10**		

Figure 2.1 *Percentage identified as slow learners or with little maths ability at seven by numeracy at 37*

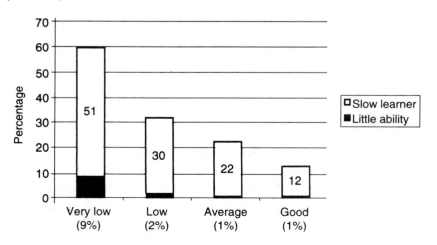

A series of multiple regression analyses of data in the two cohorts demonstrated the circumstances and experiences earlier in life that impacted on the numeracy performance of adults. What, in combination, do all these experiences tell us about the origins of numeracy difficulties?

The technical details need not concern us here, but basically multiple regression enables us to do two things. The first outcome from multiple regression analysis is a measure of how strongly each of the early influences relate to the later outcome – the adult literacy or numeracy score, *holding constant* the effects of all other influences. Secondly it tells us how much of the variation between individuals in an outcome measure, such as a numeracy score, can be predicted or accounted for, in terms of the influences to which people have been subjected, such as circumstances at home and experiences at school. The answer is given in terms of a single 'multiple correlation coefficient' (R), which is similar to the simple correlation coefficient giving the strength of relationship between two variables. R^2 tells us the percentage of variation in adult numeracy scores that can be predicted or 'explained' from the combination of other variables in the analysis.

Figure 2.2 shows that even at birth a small percentage of variation in numeracy scores can be explained by circumstances prevailing at this time. From then on the percentage of variation explained increases rapidly through primary school and then levels off by the end of compulsory education, age 16. This was the last set of circumstances available for BCS70 cohort members. For NCDS cohort members experiences and circumstances could be explored up to age 33. At every age the percentage of variation explained was higher by two or three per cent for numeracy than for literacy, indicating (at least in terms of the kinds of explanatory variables measured) that numeracy was the more sensitive to early influences of the kind measured, i.e. it was more easily explained.

Although by the standards of research of this kind a remarkably large proportion of the variability in adult basic skill scores – approaching 45 per cent – could be attributed to prior conditions and experiences, the fact that over 55 per cent remained 'unexplained' suggests that at the individual level there is still much to play for. In other words, the influences

Figure 2.2 *Percentage of variation in adult numeracy scores explained at different ages*

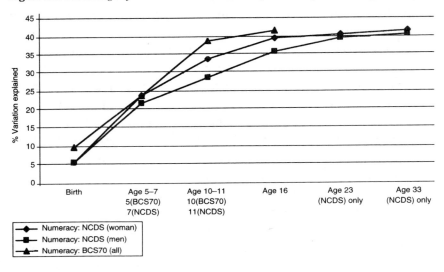

identified through our regression analyses indicated broad statistical tendencies for certain life factors and basic skills acquisition to go together. But these in themselves cannot encompass all the variety of individual adult life patterns through which school-based basic skills problems may be overcome.

As noted earlier, the multiple regression analysis also helps us to identify the key influences on basic skills development at different stages of life and provides pointers to the kinds of processes that can enhance or impede their acquisition. These are summarized in Table 2.4 together with targets for intervention.

The targets reflect the key influences on the development of numeracy at different stages of life. The combination of a disadvantaged home background and low parental engagement with education underpins a numeracy deficit which has emerged by the time the children of such families arrive at school. The main mediator of these effects is, first, poor visual-motor skills and, subsequently, poor maths attainment through the stages of schooling. Reversal of the process is targeted remediation to halt the cyclical process involved.

Labour market consequences

So, we know the background to poor adult numeracy, but what of the consequences for men and women in the labour market? We need to know whether literacy is the fundamental problem which overrides any effects of poor numeracy, or whether numeracy represents a significant problem in its own right. Given their much longer exposure to the labour market, we concentrate on the NCDS cohort.

In *Does Numeracy Matter?* (Bynner and Parsons, 1997b) a four-fold typology was developed, reflecting the different combinations of numeracy and literacy deficit and competence:

1. poor numeracy/poor literacy;
2. poor numeracy/competent literacy;
3. competent numeracy/poor literacy; and
4. competent numeracy/competent literacy.

'Very low' numeracy scores were used to define the 'poor' numeracy group. As a result of the relatively small numbers with very low literacy, the 'poor' literacy group was defined as people with 'very low' or 'low' literacy scores (about 20 per cent of the range of scores). Those cohort members with relatively high numeracy or literacy scores on this criterion were defined as 'competent'. Table 2.5 shows the percentages of male and female cohort members falling into each of these four categories. Eleven per cent fall into the poor numeracy/competent literacy category (slightly more women than men), and seven per cent fall into the competent numeracy/poor literacy category. Notably, three-quarters of men and two-thirds of women were competent in both skills.

For the purposes of most of the analysis reported here, we extrapolate from this comprehensive classification details of the employment characteristics of men and women in the two highlighted groups in Table 2.5. Do men and women with poor numeracy (former group) have more difficulty entering and holding on to employment in comparison with men and women with poor literacy (latter group), and how might it affect their prospects when in jobs?

Table 2.4 *Origins of numeracy difficulties and targets for intervention*

Life stage	Critical factors	Main outcomes	Intervention targets
Pre-school	Disadvantaged home background	Visual motor skills weak	Pre-school preparation
		Limited vocabulary	
	Parents' education poor		Family disadvantage
	No pre-school preparation – mother not reading to child		
Early primary school	Visual motor skills poor	Maths skills weak	
	Disadvantaged home background		
	Parents' interest low		Primary curriculum
			Family disadvantage
			Family literacy
			Home school relations
Late primary school	Cognitive skills weak	Maths skills weak	
	Disadvantaged home background		Pupil/teacher ratio
	Parents' interest low		
Early secondary school	Disadvantaged home background	Maths skills weak	
		Examination potential low	
	Mathematics poor		Secondary curriculum
	Non-exam/low-level exams		School/class organization
	Behaviour problems		Examinations policy

Table 2.4 *Origins of numeracy difficulties and targets for intervention* – contd

Life stage	Critical factors	Main outcomes	Intervention targets
Early secondary school *contd*	Parent interest low		Home/school relations
Late secondary school	Mathematics poor	Maths skills weak	Student behaviour
	School attendance poor	Public examinations not taken	Teacher expectations
	Behaviour problems		
	Teacher expectations low		
Post-16	Basic skills poor	Maths skills weak	Further ed. curriculum
	Early leaving full-time education	No academic qualifications	Youth training
	No qualifications	No vocational qualifications	First employment
	No work-based training		Work-based training
	Unemployment		Employers
			Unemployment
			Leisure life
Adulthood	Numeracy poor	Numeracy poor	Basic skills education
	No further education or training	No further vocational qualifications	Further education and training
	No continuous employment	No professional qualifications	Work-based training
			Unemployment
	Unemployment		Parent education

Table 2.5 *Performance in numeracy and literacy assessments at age 37*

Skill level	Overall %	Men %	Women %
1. Poor numeracy + poor literacy	12	9	15
2. Poor numeracy + competent literacy	**11**	**9**	**12**
3. Competent numeracy + poor literacy	**7**	**7**	**7**
4. Competent numeracy + competent literacy	70	75	67
Total n (100%)	**1,701**	**798**	**903**

Numeracy and employment

Figure 2.3a shows the percentages of men who were in full-time employment, unemployed, sick or other at the time of the survey.[4] Figure 2.3b shows the percentages of women in full-time or part-time employment, 'at home', sick or other at the time of the survey. Men and women showing the lowest levels of full-time labour market participation were those with poor *numeracy* rather than poor literacy. Although the vast majority of men were in full-time employment, those with poor numeracy were most prone to unemployment. A different picture was apparent for women. Notably, the women with competent numeracy and poor literacy were twice as likely as those with poor numeracy and competent literacy to be in full-time employment. Women with poor numeracy who were not in full-time employment tended to be in part-time jobs. Women with poor literacy were either in part-time jobs or engaged in 'home care'.

We see signs here of an unexpected significance attached to numeracy in holding on to jobs (part-time or full-time). More evidence for this comes from cohort members' employment histories. How does the picture change across a working life since leaving school?

Figures 2.4a and 2.4b show for men and women respectively, the percentages in full time employment at each age from 17 to the time of their thirty-seventh birthday. Notably for men, from the age of 18 until 30 the full-time employment levels of those with poor numeracy were some way below the level for the poor literacy group. In other words, poor numeracy appeared to represent the bigger problem for maintaining full-

Figure 2.3a *Current employment status of men at 37*

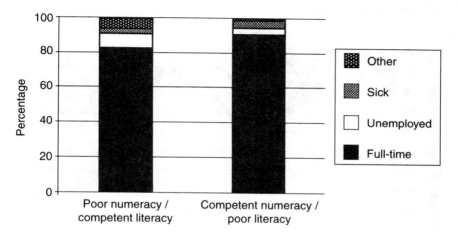

Figure 2.3b *Current employment status of women at 37*

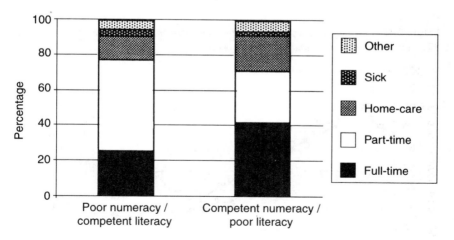

Figure 2.4a *Percentage of men in full-time employment between the ages of 17 and 37 by combined numeracy and literacy scores at 37*

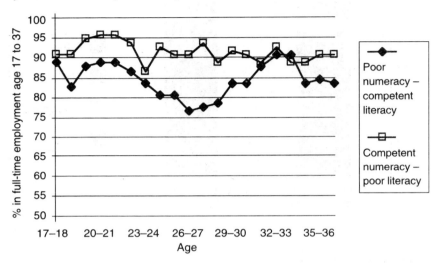

Figure 2.4b *Percentage of women in full-time employment between the ages of 17 and 37 by combined numeracy and literacy scores at 37*

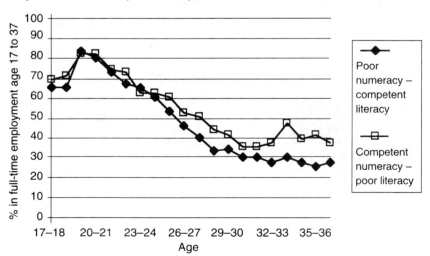

time employment than poor literacy. From the age of 31 onwards the paths of the two groups were closer, with the employment level of men with poor numeracy rising to levels just below those of men with poor literacy.

For women the impact of poor numeracy was different. Those with poor numeracy did not have lower levels of full-time employment until the age of 25. From then on, however, women with poor numeracy were leaving full-time employment in much larger numbers to care for home and family, often in combination with part-time jobs (Bynner, Morphy and Parsons, 1997) than were women with poor literacy.

Occupational disadvantage
Employment status tells us something about the way numeracy and literacy difficulties impact on employability, with poor numeracy apparently constituting the bigger problem, but we need to go further to find out what other kinds of occupational disadvantage poor numeracy held. Table 2.6 shows a number of work-related characteristics compared between the two groups: the poor numeracy/competent literacy group and the competent literacy/poor numeracy group.

Table 2.6 *Labour market characteristics associated with poor numeracy*

	Men		Women	
	Poor numeracy/ competent literacy (%)	Competent numeracy/ poor literacy (%)	Poor numeracy/ competent literacy (%)	Competent numeracy/ poor literacy (%)
In a manual occupation	74	66	39	21
Received work-based training between the ages of 16 and 23	18	30	22	38
Poor weekly wage: under £200 men, under £150 women	40	35	58	30
n (100%)	72	51	91	55

What kind of job were people with poor numeracy doing? The great majority of men and a minority of women in these two groups were in manual occupations, but the proportion was substantially higher for both sexes in the poor numeracy/competent literacy group (three-quarters for men and more than one-third for women). Common occupations for men in the poor numeracy groups were the building trades, warehouse work, plant- and machine-operative work and driving. Women were concentrated in a few personal service occupations such as waitress, hairdressing or cleaning, clerical/secretarial and sales. Clearly all these occupations present numeracy demands, raising the question of whether many of the employees are adequately equipped for them.

One of the most significant effects of poor basic skills, demonstrated in earlier reports, has been the restriction they place on access to further education, and later, to work-based training (Ekinsmyth and Bynner, 1994; Bynner and Parsons, 1997). This is due in large part to the kinds of low-grade, often part-time, work towards which people with poor basic skills gravitate. However, when training is on offer in employment, there is an added problem in taking advantage of it when proficiency in numeracy (and literacy) is poor. Again the question arises as to whether it is difficulty with numeracy or difficulty with literacy that has most effect on participation in training. Another indication of labour market disadvantage was the relative lack of work-based training for the poor numeracy group – only two-fifths of both sexes had received it, compared with almost three-fifths of those with competent numeracy and poor literacy.

Jobs that provide training offer prospects of improved income and promotion. To what extent were these facets of occupation related to numeracy problems? To control the effects of extended education on earnings, this comparison was restricted to those in full-time employment who had left school at the age of 16. Wages were depressed for the poor numeracy group, with lower rates of pay being paid to both sexes for those with poor numeracy, compared with those with poor literacy. In contrast, for promotion literacy appeared to have the more important role.

Overall, these findings reinforce the earlier conclusion that poor numeracy constitutes a disadvantage in relation to access to the labour market and success within it, over and above the disadvantage associated with poor literacy. Whatever the reasons for this, clearly raising the numeracy skills of these target populations in the least successful areas of the labour market, must be a priority.

In summary, both men and women lacking numeracy skills, compared with those lacking literacy skills, were more likely in their early careers to have been out of the full-time labour market, and engaged in low-grade work in unskilled manual jobs without training and with low pay. Of course, it would be wrong to conclude that everybody with a numeracy problem is going to have employment difficulties. In Britain's unregulated labour market, perhaps more than most others, when the economy is booming, there are numerous employment opportunities where educational handicaps embodied in basic skills deficits are no impediment to entry or advancement. What we can conclude more confidently is that those with numeracy problems are going to feel the squeeze most when the economy contracts. And as the nature of employment changes, these are the workers who are going to have to struggle hardest to obtain and hold on to jobs, and to advance their positions in them. In order to 'level the playing field', the numeracy skills of this target group clearly need to be raised.

The other side of the coin

So we know that poor numeracy reduces employment opportunities, but to what extent does the reverse effect apply? Do numeracy skills get worse in response to poor labour market experience? More specifically, in relation to our 37 year olds, have those with poor numeracy always had a problem or has time spent out of the labour market added to their difficulties? Most people do not forget how to read, to follow written instructions or to add up simple numbers, although more complex numerical skills are undoubtedly more vulnerable to 'memory loss'. Unless used and practised during adulthood, the ability to work out percentages or calculate the cubic capacity of a room, for example, are often relegated to 'something I could do when I was at school'. We need to find out to what extent these effects do extend to the skills on which the more complex ones are founded: the basics of numeracy. 'If you do not *use* it, do you *lose* it?'

As we know, maths performance at the age of 16 is a strong predictor of numeracy performance at the age of 37, even though the maths test at 16 was different in form and content from the functional numeracy test at 37. The maths test at 16 was primarily designed to assess the full range of ability, whereas the numeracy test was designed principally to identify people with very weak skills. Given this much lower 'ceiling' in the test at the age of 37, direct measures of skills 'improvement' or 'loss' between the ages of 16 and 37 were difficult to obtain. The 16 year mathematics scores were classified as 'poor' (20 per cent) versus 'competent' (80 per cent). This compares with the equivalent categorization for the 37-year numeracy score of 23 per cent ('very low' or 'poor') versus 77 per cent ('competent'). However, it should be borne in mind that these two percentages do not signify equivalence in terms of the skills level attained.

The aim of the analysis was to show how the mean (average) numeracy score at 37 changed in accordance with the amount of time spent out of paid employment for the different skills groups as defined by the maths score at 16. Given that the amount of time spent in the labour market is highly dependent on the age when leaving full-time education, the initial analysis therefore was restricted to early school leavers, i.e. the maximum working time available was 21 years (n = 595). To take account of the time women spend out of the labour market having and bringing up children, the sample of women was further restricted to those who had at least one child by the age of 37 (85 per cent of the early school leavers) – 302 men and 245 women. Time out of the labour market was measured in months, as obtained from the complete employment histories back to the age of 16 that cohort members supplied.

If time out of paid employment in these restricted samples does have a detrimental impact on an individual's basic skills, we would expect the mean numeracy score at the age of 37 to decline in accordance with time spent out of paid employment. Men and women who have amassed most time out of the labour market should have the lowest scores. Inevitably, relatively small numbers had spent large amounts of time out of paid employment (more than five years for men, more than 14 years for women) which reduces the reliability of the mean scores at these extremes.

Figures 2.5a and 2.5b show how the mean numeracy score at the age of 37 changes with the amount of time spent out of employment, for the different maths skills groups at 16 for men and women respectively. Exactly in line with prediction, the more months out of paid employment, the more the mean numeracy score declined, whatever the level of maths that had been reached at 16. For men overall and the group with 'good' numeracy scores at the age of 16, the decline in mean numeracy scores began after one year out of the labour market. For those who were in the 'poor' numeracy group at 16 the decline began immediately; with every month out of the labour market, these men's mean scores declined.

Figure 2.5a *Average numeracy score at the age of 37 by time out of paid employment between the ages of 16 and 37; men who left full-time education at 16 by their maths at 16*

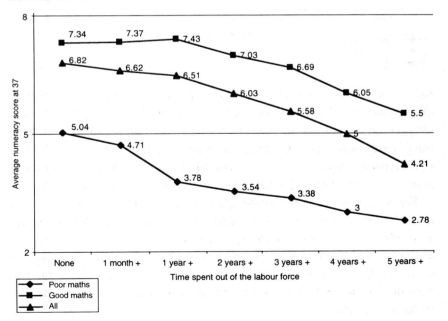

Figure 2.5b *Average numeracy score at the age of 37 by time out of paid employment between the ages of 16 and 37; women who left full-time education at 16 by their maths at 16*

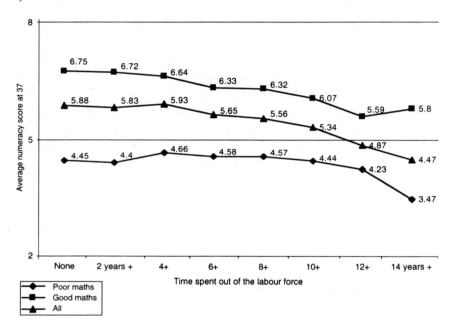

Very few women with children had not spent some time out of paid employment by the time they were 37 (n = 29). Therefore, we compare average difference scores between women who had all spent some time out of paid employment, between one month and 14 or more years. Months out of paid employment were associated with a decline in women's numeracy skills, but to a smaller extent than was the case for men.

For women with 'good' numeracy at the age of 16, a steady decline in mean scores was evident immediately. Conversely, a decline in scores was only really evident for women with poor numeracy once more than ten years had been spent without paid employment. It seems possible, therefore, that women who need and use their numeracy skills in the jobs they do, lose them to a limited extent through lack of practice when out of the labour market.

Relationship between scores at the age of 37 and time out of paid employment

The graphs provide evidence of a relationship or *correlation* between time out of paid employment and lower scores in the basic skills assessments at the age of 37 – the longer the time out, the lower the numeracy score. However, we need to apply a more rigorous test to the data and examine what else might explain why men and women who had spent the most time out of employment between the ages of 16 and 37 achieve the lowest scores in the numeracy test at 37. For example, age of leaving full-time education and exam success at 16 impact on the adult numeracy score and the amount of time spent in or out of employment.

As for the examination of early influences on adult numeracy score, multiple regression was used to find out how much of the variation in the scores obtained by men and women in the literacy and numeracy tests at the age of 37 could be accounted for by other factors, i.e. to what extent can we explain how one person gets a higher score than another. We can also say how strong the relationship is between each of these 'explanatory' influences and literacy and numeracy at 37, while holding constant the effect of all the other possible influences.

The other factors in this instance are individual scores in the reading or maths test at the age of 16 and the amount of time the respondent had spent out of paid employment. They also embrace a number of family background circumstances and employment experiences between the ages of 16 and 37. We use the whole sample for this analysis, i.e. the cohort members who completed tests at both 16 and 37: n = 1286 in all, but carry it out separately for the groups with 'good' or 'poor' maths scores at 16.

Table 2.7 confirms the earlier picture obtained from the graphs. Even when controlling for all the other influences for men and women with poor or good skills at the age of 16, the longer the time out of employment the lower the numeracy score. This effect remained particularly strong for the numeracy scores of men with a poor grasp of maths at the age of 16. In contrast, for men and women with a good understanding of maths at 16, time out of paid employment lost much of its impact on their numeracy at 37. Over and above all the other influences, the more time people spent out of employment the more their basic skills deteriorated. However, the relationship was weaker. In other words, when we take account of these other influences the damaging effect of absence from the labour market is slightly less evident. This supports our earlier conclusion that poor skills are more susceptible than good skills to further deterioration if they are under-utilized.

Table 2.7 *Influence of maths skills at 16 and time spent out of paid employment on numeracy at the age of 37 – controlling for demographic and post-16 experiences*

		Men			Women	
	All	Poor maths at 16	Good maths at 16	All	Poor maths at 16	Good maths at 16
Maths score at 16	.48[1]	.22[4]	.33[1]	.51[1]	.30[1]	.44[1]
Time out of paid employment	−.11[2]	−.15	−.09[4]	−.06	−.18[3]	−.02
Social class at birth	−.02	.16	−.05*	.08[3]	.17[4]	.07[4]
Age left full-time education	.24[1]	.05	.29[1]	.07	.03	.06
Number of children at 37	.02	.05	.02	.03	.05	.02
Work related training 16–23	.03	.11	.02	.05	.18[3]	.03
Work related training 23–33	.03	.15	.02	.12[1]	.11	.14[2]
R	**.61[1]**	**.47[1]**	**.50[1]**	**.62[1]**	**.46[1]**	**.55[1]**
R²	**38%**	**22%**	**25%**	**38%**	**21%**	**30%**

Notes: [1]p<.001; [2]p<.01; [3]p<.05; [4]p<.1 (not statistically significant).
          * The relationship is in the 'wrong' direction.

What role do the other background circumstances and experiences have in relation to the problem? The fact that when all these factors are taken into account, the overall predictability of the scores improves, and the fact that the relationship between time out of employment and the literacy and numeracy scores is weakened, suggests that these other factors are having a significant impact. A higher social class at birth, for example, has a positive impact on the scores at the age of 37 for those with poor skills at the age of 16, particularly among women. Although this aspect of an individual's life cannot be changed, it is clear that the basic skills of those brought up in more disadvantaged circumstances are more adversely affected: middle-class homes provide a degree of protection. Work-related training is another good positive predictor of 37-year numeracy scores for men and women with poor maths skills at 16. It suggests that such training can also offer a degree of protection against the adverse effects of time out of the labour market for people with poor numeracy.

Conclusion

We started this chapter by raising the question whether poor adult numeracy was an important issue for adults, compared with poor literacy. The survey gives striking evidence that numeracy *does* matter. People without numeracy skills suffered greater disadvantage in employment than those with poor literacy skills alone. They left school early, frequently without qualifications, and had more difficulty in getting and maintaining full-time employment. The jobs entered were generally low grade with limited training opportunities and poor pay and prospects. Women with numeracy difficulties appeared especially vulnerable to exclusion from the clerical and sales jobs to which they aspired. Men's problems were less clearly differentiated between occupations.

The numeracy problem begins early in disadvantaged family circumstances and carries over into problems with keeping up at school. Teachers seemed relatively inefficient at identifying incipient numeracy problems. Large numbers of children, who subsequently had numeracy problems as adults, had failed to have their problems recognized while they were at school. Recognition of childhood literacy problems was more evident, although large numbers of children were still falling through the net.

In the modern state few people can escape using literacy skills, so there is a continual challenge to maintain and improve them. This is less the case for numeracy. Those without numeracy skills are likely to be located in areas of the job market where they are often not under such pressure to exercise numeracy skills, and probably avoid situations in every day life where such skills might be needed. Consequently, when people with poor numeracy are out of the labour market, they may find their skills deteriorate even further. This may account for part of the gap between teachers' perceptions of maths problems at school and numeracy competence in adulthood as revealed by test scores.

Whether or not the gap can be accounted for in these terms, there is clearly a need to improve the skills of teachers (and parents) in monitoring children's educational progress and taking the appropriate remedial action when difficulties with the basic skills begin to emerge. Such monitoring is clearly necessary through primary school, but is also important over the crucial period from 13 onwards when young people begin to form their ideas about possible jobs. In adult life, the need for remedial teaching for those with poor numeracy gains added impetus from this research.

One feature of the modern labour market is the relentless decline in unskilled and partly skilled occupations of the kind our 'typical' poor numeracy cohort members were engaged in (Industry in Education, 1997). As the number of such occupations declines further, the people in them face increasing risk of unemployment. Moreover Britain tends to fare badly compared with other countries on these kinds of numeracy skills (International Numeracy Survey, 1997).

As the last part of the chapter demonstrated, unemployment impacts negatively on numeracy skills. The longer the absence from paid employment between the ages of 16 and 37, the greater the negative impact on their numeracy scores. The impact of time out of paid employment on 37-year numeracy scores is strongest when maths attainment is poor at the age of 16, which suggests that once a certain maths threshold has been attained at school, skills are protected from the effects of absence from paid employment. To improve opportunities to get jobs, numeracy skills at the bottom end need to be enhanced. This argues for viewing numeracy as just as important a target for educational intervention with adults as literacy.

Notes

1. We wish to acknowledge the support of the Basic Skills Agency, the predecessor to the Adult Literacy and Basic Skills Unit, who funded the research reported here. However, the views expressed are those of the authors. We also acknowledge the National Child Development Study (NCDS) and the 1970 British Cohort Study (BCS70) cohort members who have participated in the studies reported here since they were born, and their long-term funders: the Economic and Social Research Council and numerous government departments and agencies.

2. Foundation level numeracy broadly corresponds to levels 3 and 4 of the mathematics National Curriculum. Numeracy level 2 is a level below GCSE grade C in mathematics

3. At age seven (1965): *Southgate Reading Test* (Southgate, 1962), a test of word recognition and comprehension particularly suited to identifying backward readers; *Problem Arithmetic Test* (Pringle et al., 1966).

   At age 11 (1969): *Reading Comprehension Test*, constructed by the National Foundation for Educational Research in England and Wales (NFER) specifically for use in this study. *Arithmetic/Mathematics Test* was also constructed by NFER specifically for use in this study.

   At age 16 (1974): *Reading Comprehension Test* – the same test as at age 11; *Mathematics Test*, devised at the University of Manchester. (Tests not referenced have not been published. Copies are available from the Centre for Longitudinal Studies, Institute of Education, University of London, 20 Bedford Way, London, WC1H 0AL.)

4. For men, 'other' = part-time employment, home care, education/training; for women 'other' = unemployment, education/training. 'Sickness' is defined as a temporary or permanent state – an absence of at least six months on a continuous basis from the labour market. Forty-four people were permanently sick. This group included five men and three women who had never worked on a full-time basis. All others had a self-reported sickness which had taken them out of the labour market at some stage in their employment careers. Some of this illness may be masking actual unemployment.

3 The Pay-off to Mathematics A Level[1]

Peter J. Dolton and Anna F. Vignoles

Institute of Education and University of Newcastle upon Tyne; and Centre for Economic Performance, London School of Economics and Political Science

Introduction

Following the recent Dearing review of 16–19 qualifications (Dearing, 1996), and after much public debate, the A level system is to be reformed. From September 2000, students will be expected to follow a broader curriculum, which will also place a greater emphasis on certain key skills such as numeracy. An important question, which we have addressed in some recent research (Dolton and Vignoles, 1998, 1999), is whether these reforms will actually benefit students and provide employers with the skills they require. The more specific issue that is discussed here is whether improving students' advanced mathematics skills is likely to make individuals more productive in the work place and hence benefit them economically. The main conclusion from our research is that there is a high wage premium associated with having a mathematics A level. This suggests that improving students' *advanced* mathematics skills will boost their productivity and earnings. However, as the proposed key skills course for 16–19 year olds only includes a section on the 'application of number', which covers a relatively low level mathematics curriculum,[2] there is no guarantee that this will necessarily improve the productivity and earnings of the students who take it.

Mathematics within the changing post-16 curriculum

The reform of the A level system

Many critics of A levels believe that reform of the system is long overdue. Dating as far back as the Crowther Report in 1959, A levels have been criticized on the grounds that they do not necessarily provide an appropriate and balanced curriculum for 16–19 year olds. In particular, various reports have suggested that the average A level curriculum is too specialized and, more specifically, that A levels do not give students the key skills they need for the world of work (DES, Higginson Report, 1988; Institute for Public Policy Research, 1990). When consulted during Dearing's review of 16–19 qualifications (1996), many employers and universities expressed concerns about students' lack of key skills. More specifically, some university departments were very concerned about the low standard of numeracy and mathematics of some students.[3] Although key skills are already an important part of the National Curriculum, and therefore should be developed during the compulsory schooling phase, the need to further develop these skills at 16–19 is seen as crucial by many. This need was certainly a decisive factor behind some of Dearing's recommendations for reforming A levels.[4] The impetus for reform has also grown as the number of students taking these qualifications has increased.

Dearing (1996) succeeded, at least partially, in pressing the case for some reform. He recommended that the basic A level be kept, but that the AS level be reformed and that greater curriculum breadth at 16–19 be introduced. The government has endorsed only some of Dearing's recommendations. It has remained firmly committed to the 'gold standard' of A levels, although students will now be encouraged to take up to five different subjects in their first year of the sixth form, in addition to a key skills course in information technology (IT), communication and the 'application of number'. Specifically, at the end of their first year in sixth form, pupils will take up to *five* reformed AS level examinations, with the option of taking a key skills qualification which will have the same weight, in terms of UCAS points, as an AS level. However, as has already been said, the mathematical curriculum content of this key skills qualification is relatively low level: apparently closer to GCSE level than AS level.

A level mathematics and employment

The success of these reforms will depend on many factors, not least of which is the cooperation of higher education institutions in changing their entry requirements, and the willingness of students to take the (voluntary) options recommended by the government. A related issue is whether the reforms will actually meet the needs of employers and improve students' work prospects. We investigated this directly by evaluating the effect of taking different A levels on students' later earnings, and assessing whether students with A level mathematics skills earn significantly more than their peers. The specific issue of advanced mathematical skills was certainly of great concern to Dearing who, given the recent evidence of a decline in the proportion of students taking mathematics, urged for much more research into 'factors affecting the attitudes of parents, pupils and teachers to mathematics and the sciences'.[5] Clearly the tangible financial benefits of taking advanced mathematics, in terms of higher wages, will affect attitudes towards the subject. Quantifying the impact of A level mathematics on pupils' later earnings may also give us an idea of the likely impact of adding a key skills qualification in the 'application of number' to the 16–19 curriculum. However, as we were only able to investigate the impact of taking A level mathematics on individuals' subsequent pay, and the proposed key skills qualification is of a lower mathematical standard, caution must be exercised when applying our research results to this issue.

Advanced mathematics and individual development

We took a relatively narrow economic perspective in our research, focusing only on the *labour market* value of specific advanced mathematics skills, i.e. those developed by taking mathematics A level (see also Murnane, Willett and Levy, 1995). The reason for this approach is that the needs of employers have been cited repeatedly as the prime motivation behind the imminent reforms to the A level system. As Dearing himself put it:

> Education and training are central to the prospects of today's young
> people for earning a good standard of living … . The only strategy for
> a nation seeking to maintain and enhance a high standard of living, lies

in concentration on advanced products and services, a high level of innovation, challenging and constantly improving standards of achievement and competitiveness, based on a highly educated, well-trained and adaptable workforce.   (Dearing, 1996: 3)

Therefore, it is entirely appropriate to try to predict the likely effect of these reforms on pupils' labour market progress. However, education is obviously not undertaken merely to improve earnings. Education is valuable as an end in itself, and the financial benefit of a particular academic subject is clearly just one of the criteria that should be used to determine the appropriate curriculum for pupils. Notwithstanding this, it could be argued that mathematics, due to the nature of the skills (numeracy, deductive reasoning, mental agility, etc.) that it develops, is of the greatest importance in terms of its impact on individuals' lives. For example, mathematics develops children's critical reasoning and, thus, can enhance their ability to understand the world around them and build their confidence. Although this chapter addresses the narrower question of whether there is a pay-off to advanced mathematics skills, these broader issues are obviously of equal importance.

The narrow focus of A levels

Before considering the specific issue of mathematics A level, we first discuss some of the problems associated with the A level system in general. The advantages of A levels are numerous, and have been well publicized by those who favour the traditional A level system. First and foremost, A levels are perceived by employers and students alike as being rigorous and there is a high degree of public confidence in their standards. This has ensured that A levels attract a significant wage premium in the labour market. Evidence suggests that in their early 20s, for example, workers with A levels earn approximately eight–20 per cent more than those without any qualifications (Dearden, Ferri and Meghir, 1998).[6] However, A levels were initially developed as university entrance examinations.[7] Thus, their narrow focus is partly the result of the specific purpose for which they were originally designed, i.e. to determine whether or not a student was competent to continue on to higher education. It has long been recognised that they may consequently not provide a suitable curriculum for students who do not go on to higher education. Also, as students choose their own subjects at A level, not all of them necessarily reach the same standard in some key skills, such as numeracy and literacy.

Mathematics A level entries

The number of students taking A levels has risen dramatically, particularly in the last decade, as illustrated in Figure 3.1. For example, just 20 per cent of English 17–18 year olds took A levels in 1986, but by 1997 this had grown to over one-third of the cohort. Certainly today A levels are the most common route into higher education. However, within this great expansion at A level, there are some concerning trends. The free choice given to students at A level has meant that a large proportion of students has been able to drop science and mathematics altogether at the age of 16. Table 3.1 shows that in 1997 only nine per cent of all A level entries were in mathematics and 21 per cent in science. This compares to the growing popularity of social science and arts subjects, which together constituted nearly half of all A level entries last year. Furthermore, much of the recent expansion of A levels has been in non-scientific subjects, an issue of great concern to Dearing (1996) and others.

Figure 3.1 *Percentage of English 17-year-old cohort with one or more A levels or AS equivalent, 1986–1998*

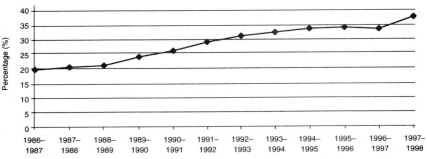

Source: DES/DfEE Education Statistics (annual).

Table 3.1 *A-level subject entries, 1997*

Subject	No. of entries	Proportion (%)
Science	150,547	21
Mathematics	63,858	9
Social science	216,415	30
Arts	121,250	17
English	89,043	13
General studies	72,456	10
Total no. of entries	**713,569**	**100**

Note: This table includes all candidates in schools or Further Education colleges.
Source: Department for Education and Employment, Education Statistics, 1997.

Even more worrying perhaps, is the long-term downward trend in the numbers taking mathematics, although this decline appears to have levelled out in recent years (Schools Curriculum Assessment Authority, 1996; Department for Education and Employment, 1997). Figure 3.2 shows the steady decline in the size of the mathematics A level candidature between 1989 and 1995. Over this period, there was a 24 per cent drop in the numbers taking mathematical subjects. However, over this period there was also a 25 per cent fall in cohort size. Hence the proportion of the age cohort with mathematics A level has remained stable over this time. Given the upward trend in the percentage of the cohort with *any* A level subject, the lack of any increase in the incidence of those taking mathematics is of potential concern. This, and concerns expressed by employers about the difficulty of recruiting individuals with good mathematics skills, was the prime motivation behind Dearing's recommendation that further research be carried out into the declining popularity of mathematics and some other science subjects.

Figure 3.2 *Total number of A level candidates in mathematics, 1989–1995*

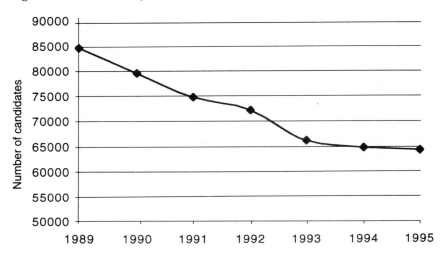

Source: GCE Results Analysis: An analysis of the 1995 GCE results and trends over
         time 1989–1995. Figures refer to England, Wales and Northern Ireland.

The pay-off to mathematics A level

Research focus

Standard economic theory suggests that if there is a shortage of a particular
skill, then individuals who possess this skill will earn more than those
who do not, at least in the short run. Over the longer term, of course, one
would expect the higher earnings associated with a particular skill to provide an incentive for individuals to invest in the education or training
needed to acquire that skill. This in turn will increase the supply of the
skill, and reduce the wage premium associated with it. So one way to
verify whether there is really a shortage of higher level mathematics
skills is to assess whether employers pay a wage premium for workers
who have mathematics A Level. This was one of the purposes of our
research.

During the course of our investigation, we examined the impact of
A level subjects on the labour market success of several different groups

of workers, from a number of different surveys. Indeed, one difficulty we faced was finding appropriate data on which to base our research. Many of the most detailed educational data sets contain good information on the A level subjects taken by students, but once the students leave education and enter the labour market they tend not to be followed up (e.g. the A Level Information System surveys). Equally, most of the surveys that are oriented towards obtaining labour market information do not contain full information on the different subjects that individuals took at A level (e.g. the British Household Panel Survey). Finding up-to-date and comprehensive information on A level subjects and labour market progress proved difficult. This paucity of information perhaps reflects the fact that, whilst many researchers have studied the effect of taking A levels on various pupil outcomes, very few have investigated the impact of different A level *subjects* on outcomes. To overcome these data difficulties, we used a number of different surveys to cross check our findings.

The data

First, we used data from the National Child Development Study (NCDS).[8] This is a longitudinal study that surveyed a sample of all the children born in the UK in one particular week in March 1958. Since then five full follow-up surveys have been undertaken when the subjects were aged seven, 11, 16, 23 and 33. The original 1958 NCDS target sample was approximately 17,000, although only 15,500 babies and their parents actually participated in the first survey. However, we used information from the 1991 survey, by which time the sample had been reduced to 11,500. Extensive work has been completed by other researchers investigating the representative nature of the NCDS sample (Ferri, 1993) and the sample from the 1991 survey has been compared to earlier samples in the study. There does appear to have been a significant loss of non-whites and immigrants from the sample. However the NCDS sample has also been compared to other UK surveys such as the General Household Survey and has been found to be broadly representative.

As the NCDS study has monitored these individuals throughout their lives, we now have a very comprehensive profile of their childhood experiences, education and progress in the labour market. The richness of the information on this group of workers enabled us to identify the key factors that affected these individuals' earnings at the age of 33. Obviously, someone's earnings are influenced by a multitude of different factors, such as how much work experience they have, how long they have been in their job, their gender and where they live. Another most important factor which affects earnings is an individual's overall level of education. In our sample, workers with a degree, for example, earned up to 20 per cent more than those with just A levels. However, we were most interested in the effect of particular curriculum options on earnings, rather than the effect of overall education level. Therefore, we just looked at a group of workers who had at least one A level and then modelled the effect of taking particular A level subjects on earnings. In general, those who studied science, a foreign language or English at A level earned no more (and no less) than workers who had taken other subjects at A level. In fact, we concluded that the specific curriculum studied at A level had little effect on earnings,[9] except for mathematics which adds around seven to ten per cent to earnings. In other words, if you take a group of workers who have A levels, only those with mathematics A level earn systematically more than average.

Further investigation of the 'mathematics premium'

As we have already discussed, we could not find the perfect data with which to address this issue. One problem with using the NCDS sample is that a very large proportion of the women with A levels or degrees (around 55 per cent) were not in full time employment at the age 33. Most of the women who were not employed were out of the labour force altogether, rather than in full-time study or unemployed. This causes some technical problems when trying to model the factors that influence their earnings.[10] To overcome this problem, we also investigated the impact of A level mathematics on the earnings of a group of young graduates. These graduates left higher education in 1980 and were followed up six years after graduation. They were asked detailed questions about many aspects of their lives, particularly their educational and labour market history. We found that amongst this group of workers, female graduates with mathematics A level earned on average ten per cent more than those who had taken other A level subjects. Male graduates with mathematics A level earned seven per cent more than those without. This means that if one observes two graduates, with similar backgrounds and with the *same degree subject*, one finds that the person who took mathematics A level earns around ten per cent more than the one who did not. This result is all the more remarkable given that all of this second group of workers had at least a degree, and one might expect that particular A level subjects would make little difference to the earnings of graduates.

'Value-added' analysis

When we carried out our research, using both the NCDS and the graduate samples, we attempted to allow for as many factors as possible when trying to identify the effect of A level mathematics on earnings. Therefore, we investigated the effect of mathematics A level on earnings, for different types of individuals, in various different situations. Of greatest concern to us was to allow for the initial ability of each individual, i.e. their ability prior to starting their A level curriculum. Otherwise, as is discussed further below, we might just be picking up a 'signalling effect' from the fact that more able students are more likely to choose to take mathematics at A level. We were able to allow for the separate effects of ability and other factors, as opposed to A level curriculum, in a number of ways. In particular, with the NCDS data we estimated a 'value-added' type model, allowing for the individual's ability, achievements and background *prior* to starting their A level course. We even allowed for their O level mathematics grade. Even taking into account all these factors, we still found a positive effect on earnings from taking mathematics A level of between seven and ten per cent. Other important results that we found are that even those who got relatively low grades in mathematics earned more than other people who had taken different subjects at A level. Furthermore, in the NCDS sample A level mathematics still had a positive effect for graduates, as well as non-graduates. The positive effect from having mathematics A level was also evident, regardless of the occupation that the person chose to work in. In other words, even when considering two graduate managers who had taken the same degree subject and who had similar backgrounds, it would still be the case that if one of them had mathematics A level then that person would earn more than the one without.

Critique

A final word of caution must be added. As economists, we are primarily interested in the effect of education on earnings. To study this relationship properly, we must evaluate the impact of specific educational options on the earnings of workers who have been in the labour market for some time. In our case, we looked at workers in their late 20s and early 30s. Inevitably, this means that we are measuring the effects of education that was acquired up to two decades ago. This raises two problems.

The first problem is that the curriculum content of A levels may have changed since that time. As Figure 3.1 shows, there was a noticeable jump in the proportion of students taking A levels in 1988–1989. This may be attributable to the replacement of O levels with General Certificates of Education (GCSEs) two years previously. It has been shown that the introduction of GCSEs led to an increase in the proportion of candidates getting good grades and staying on at school (Ashford, Gray and Tranmer, 1993). If this occurred because GCSEs are of lower academic standard, this might imply that the jump between GCSE and A level is greater than the jump between O level and A level used to be. Or, it may mean that A levels have had to be 'dumbed down' in response to the introduction of GCSEs.[11] However, the evidence is by no means clear on this. Another example is the modularization of A levels which may, via the ability to resit individual modules and the spreading of assessment over time, have led to the devaluation of A levels (this issue is discussed in more detail below and in Dearing, 1996).

The second problem is that the labour market has also changed substantially over this period. This means that our results can only provide some guidance for policy-makers, rather than any definitive estimate of the effect of taking a particular A level subject today on earnings several years hence. Nonetheless, the evidence seems powerful enough to merit it being considered carefully in the ongoing debate on A level reform.

So why do so few students take mathematics?

Perceptions of the value of mathematics A level

Given the strong evidence of the financial benefit from taking mathematics A level, an obvious question is why do more students not choose to take this subject at A level? The reasons for the low take-up of mathematics are discussed in more detail in Chapter Five. However, we also explore a number of alternative explanations here. One possibility is that the wage premium we have observed being paid to those with mathematics A Level is merely temporary. Over the longer run, we may expect more students to take mathematics A level, attracted by the higher wages on offer to those who study this subject. As the numbers with mathematics A level increased, we would expect the wage premium associated with mathematics to fall. But our research has suggested that the wage premium may be more permanent, as we found evidence of it in both the 1980s and 1990s. Thus, the reason more students do not take mathematics A level may be because the financial rewards to this qualification are hidden. Most of the students who have mathematics A level also have other qualifications, particularly degrees. Hence students may focus on acquiring the subject requirements needed to study for a particular degree subject, rather than on the A level subjects themselves. Also, most employers do not specifically include mathematics A level as a job requirement, even though they favour those with this qualification, again making it more difficult for students to evaluate the financial benefits associated with mathematics A level.

Incentives for taking mathematics A level

If students are unaware of the wage premium associated with mathematics A level, then teachers and careers services, who may themselves be unaware of the pay-off to mathematics A level, should be advising students of the benefits of this qualification, and perhaps encouraging more who are capable of studying advanced mathematics to take this subject. However, it is unlikely that encouragement alone would increase the take up of mathematics A level. If universities were to alter their educational requirements to include a key skills AS level, or if it were made mandatory for all 16–19 year olds to take some mathematics to a higher standard than GCSE, this might address the problem. Although a key skills AS level would clearly be below A level, if it were more rigorous than GCSE level it might meet at least some of the needs of firms and provide higher wages for those with these more advanced mathematics skills. However, we need to be clear that our evidence only shows the benefits of advanced mathematics. If the mathematical component of the key skills AS level was set to GCSE standard or below, this would not necessarily have any positive effect on students' labour market outcomes.

Disincentives for taking mathematics A level

An alternative explanation for why more students do not take mathematics is, however, that many students lack the preparatory knowledge required to take mathematics A level and/or perceive mathematics as a difficult subject. Table 3.2 shows the pass rate and percentage of grade As awarded in mathematics. The percentage pass rates suggest that students who take mathematics are *not* more likely to fail, as compared to those taking other subjects, and indeed a very high proportion of those taking mathematics A level end up with a grade A. Furthermore, data from the Schools Curriculum Assessment Authority (SCAA) (1996) indicates that the proportion of mathematics A level candidates awarded a grade A has actually increased over time, particularly since 1992.

This evidence, however, does not necessarily contradict the view that A level mathematics *is* a more difficult subject. If only the most able students take mathematics A level, then one would expect a high number of them to get good grades, even if mathematics is genuinely a more difficult subject. Furthermore, detailed research by Fitz-Gibbon (1985) suggests that, once students' performance at O level/GCSE is taken into account, mathematics A level is more difficult than certain other subjects, such as English A level.[12] She argues that this may put off many students

Table 3.2 *Pass rates and grade As awarded in mathematics, 1995*

Subject	Pass rate (%)	Grade A (%)
Mathematics	87	27
English	90	14
Physical science	84	21
Geography	83	13
Social science	75	11

Source: GCE results analysis: an analysis of the 1995 GCE results and trends over time, SCAA (1996). Figures refer to England, Wales and Northern Ireland.

from taking mathematics.[13] Of course, this may also be the reason why this more challenging subject attracts a higher wage premium in the first place, as we now discuss in more detail.

Is it just a signalling effect?

The evidence that mathematics is possibly a harder subject to take at A level may have implications for our results. Perhaps it is not the case that employers value mathematics skills specifically, nor that having mathematics skills actually makes individuals more productive in their jobs. Rather, as we have already mentioned, it may simply be that the most able students take mathematics and that these students are more attractive to firms. Employers may be choosing to recruit those with mathematics A level, and pay them more, not because of the curriculum choices they have made, but because they are inherently more able individuals, and their having taken mathematics A level is a signal of this ability.

Allowing for previous mathematical achievement

Certainly, we found evidence that those who are more able in mathematics and who perform better at O level are more likely to take mathematics A level. Other research has also shown that early achievement in mathematics and science is a good predictor of later curriculum choices

(Fitz-Gibbon, 1999). However, our work attempts to take account of this. When we evaluated the effect of mathematics A level on earnings, we allowed for the previous ability of the student in reading and mathematics tests at age 16 and their curriculum and performance at O level. As we have indicated, when we allowed for these factors in our model, we still found a distinct, independent effect from taking mathematics A level. This seems to confirm that, for a given level of ability, a mathematics A level curriculum leads to a higher wage than other A level subjects.[14] Another important point is that more able students are equally likely to choose certain 'difficult' science subjects, particularly physical sciences. Dearing (1996) indicated that several subjects, in addition to mathematics, may be more difficult for students, namely physics, chemistry and some modern foreign languages. In fact Fitz-Gibbon and Vincent (1994) found that physics is the 'most difficult' A level subject of all. Yet we did not find an additional positive effect on wages from taking physics, or indeed other subjects such as chemistry. This would seem to support our argument that it is the specific skills and knowledge provided by mathematics A level that attracts a wage premium in the labour market. The role of specific mathematics skills in the workplace is a complex issue that is discussed in some detail in Chapter Seven. However, evidence would seem to support the view that individuals use quite complex and abstract mathematical thinking in the workplace, a skill that may well be developed effectively via the mathematics A level curriculum.

So why is there a pay-off to mathematics A level?

Skills imparted by studying A level mathematics

To summarize our findings: the premium from A level mathematics is still evident, even when individuals have been in the labour market some time. Taking into account an array of personal characteristics and other factors such as the individual's general level of education, his or her previous ability in mathematics (and degree subject and class if he or she has one), we still find that mathematics A level boosts earnings. There are however, a number of different ways in which mathematics A level may confer a return in terms of higher earnings. Firstly, it is our hypothesis (and that of many authors in this book) that mathematics A level imparts skills which directly increase productivity in the work place, for example the ability to think logically, to solve complex problems, etc. This would explain why workers with mathematics A level are paid more, particularly if these high level skills are in relatively short supply.

Complementary skills

We must, however, acknowledge a second possibility. Individuals with good mathematical skills may also have other skills that are highly valued in the labour market. Take, for example, computing skills. These skills have been shown to be of great importance in the labour market and workers with these skills earn higher wages (Krueger, 1991; Green, 1998). In our model we are unable to measure individuals' computing skills. Hence if workers who have good computing skills also tend to have good mathematics skills, what we measure as a return to mathematics A level may in fact be a return to computing skills. As we are unable to test these individuals' computing skills, there is no real way around this problem. Of course, workers may also have other types of skills, which are related to their mathematics skills and may be causing our result. For example, if workers with more 'work intelligence' also tend, on average, to have better mathematics skills, then again what we measure as a return to mathematics A level may in fact be a return to higher 'work intelligence'. This is obviously an avenue for future research.

A level mathematics and choice of employment

Finally, workers with mathematics A level may be more likely to enter certain higher-paying occupations. We do allow for this in our research, for example by comparing the earnings of workers with and without mathematics A level *within* different occupations. However, we are only able to identify very broadly the person's occupation. We know, for example, whether he or she is in a managerial role, a technician role, doing a manual job, etc. If however, workers with mathematics A level tend to go into particular types of (higher paid) managerial roles, in particular (high paying) industries, we may be attributing workers' higher pay to their mathematics skills when in fact they are higher paid because they work in different types of jobs. Indeed, Table 3.3 suggests that those with mathematics A level are more likely to be in professional level jobs. Nonetheless, this problem does not seem to undermine our results too seriously, as one can argue that these workers' mathematics skills enabled them to get higher paid jobs in the first place. Again, this is a topic for further research.

Table 3.3 *Occupations of NCDS sample*

Occupational status (of current/latest job)	Total sample	% of total sample	Those with maths A level	% maths A level sample
Professional	241	17.88%	95	30.35%
Manager/skilled technician	796	59.05%	168	53.67%
Skilled non-manual	229	16.99%	35	11.18%
Skilled manual	43	3.19%	11	3.51%
Part skilled	38	2.82%	3	0.96%
Unskilled	1	0.07%	1	0.32%
Unknown	93	6.90%	0	0.00%
Total	**1,348**	**100.00%**	**313**	**100.00%**

Policy implications

Raising mathematical standards

Our research has a number of important policy implications. Our evidence highlights the crucial policy importance of the efforts being made to raise the standard of UK mathematics. There is now a quite considerable body of UK research that has investigated the standards achieved in mathematics, at all levels, and that has explored the importance of mathematics skills in the labour market. For example, research has highlighted the relatively poor mathematics performance of younger students in the UK (Prais, 1995).[15] Furthermore, Bynner and Parsons (1997b) have shown, as has previous research by the Basic Skills Agency (BSA), that Britain performs badly relative to other countries in terms of adult numeracy. We also know that having very poor numeracy skills continues to affect adults adversely through out their lives (Bynner and Parsons, 1998). Our results reinforce the message that numerical skills are crucial to employers and individuals alike, by illustrating the importance of *advanced* mathematical skills. Although this government is attempting to address these numeracy/ mathematics issues, the evidence suggests that are no short-run 'quick fix' solutions.[16] In policy terms, our research should encourage continued efforts to improve UK mathematics, from primary school upwards.

Encouraging participation in mathematics beyond GCSE

In terms of the current reforms to the post-16 curriculum, our evidence supports the view that more students should be encouraged to acquire advanced mathematics skills at 16–19, where possible. The move to encourage greater breadth at A level may have a positive effect in this regard.[17] If persuading students to take five subjects at AS level ensures that more of them continue to study mathematics beyond the age of 16, this is likely to have a positive effect on pupils' labour market outcomes. The introduction of a key skills qualification may also ensure that more students improve their mathematics skills post 16. However, our evidence can only predict the effects of adding *advanced* mathematical skills to the 16–19 curriculum. If the key skills qualification only includes lower level mathematical skills, it may not have such a positive effect on student outcomes. In other words, there is no guarantee that simply adding mathematics to the 16–19 curriculum will improve labour market outcomes if the academic standard of the course is not sufficiently rigorous.

Modular A levels

There are a number of different ways one might try to encourage greater take-up of mathematics at 16–19. The potential for modularization to devalue A levels has been discussed at length by many commentators, including Dearing (1996). This has resulted in attempts to limit the number of 'resits' that are allowed per module and much discussion about whether

A levels should be labelled clearly as modular or non-modular. However, more positively, modularization may provide the opportunity to tailor the A level curriculum to the particular needs of students. For example, certain aspects of the A level mathematics curriculum may be more appropriate for a student than other parts. If a student is taking mostly social science A levels for instance, he or she may benefit from focusing on the statistical aspects of the curriculum and conversely, mechanics options may be preferable for those studying the physical sciences and engineering. Modularization can allow students to specialize in aspects of the mathematics curriculum that are of greatest use/interest to them. This flexibility, if properly applied, may in turn encourage more students to take mathematics A level, particularly those who are taking other A level subjects that are outside the sciences. A related approach, designed to boost the take-up of mathematics at 16–19, is being proposed by the Qualifications and Curriculum Authority (QCA). The QCA is piloting 12 different mathematics units, which will be available to pupils from September 2000. The advanced versions of these 'stand-alone' units will equate to one A level module (there are six modules in an A level). The units will teach the principles of mathematics, but also focus on applying mathematics skills to other curriculum areas, for example science. Some will be set at GCSE mathematics standard, others at a more advanced level. These courses may well provide A level students who do not wish to take a whole A level in mathematics with at least some of the advanced mathematics skills required by employers.

In practical terms, when advising students on their curriculum options, one obviously has to consider their likelihood of success in each subject. As we have shown in this chapter, at the moment at least, individuals who take mathematics A level are no more likely to fail than those who take other subjects. However, we have also discussed the fact that A level mathematics students may, on average, be more able than those who take some other subjects. Therefore, advisors need to take this into account. It is true that even students who do relatively badly in the examination still earn a wage premium from mathematics A level. However, we should not be recommending students to take subjects that they have a high probability of failing. The failure rate in mathematics is still over ten per cent, which represents a lot of disappointment for a significant number of students. We would not want to push this figure any higher. However, our evidence does suggest that students who are capable of succeeding at mathematics A level should take this option if they wish to have greater labour market success in the future.

Effects on teacher supply

A final policy problem highlighted by our research is the issue of mathematics teaching. The difficulty of recruiting mathematics teachers is well publicized. For instance, the recent Green Paper on teachers has suggested that, whilst there is an overall shortage of secondary school teachers (relative to published recruitment targets), the shortage in mathematics is particularly serious.[18] Between 1997 and 1998 the numbers applying for postgraduate mathematics courses fell by almost 25 per cent. Although the government has been trying to address this issue in a number of ways, for example by offering 'golden hello' grants to those wishing to teach mathematics, recruitment in this area is still problematic. Our research may help explain why teacher shortages in mathematics are so severe. Previous evidence has already shown that the choice of teaching as a career is influenced by the relative wage rate of teachers (Dolton, 1990). As our results suggest that those with A level mathematics earn a large wage premium for their subject, this is likely to make it even more difficult for the teaching profession to attract mathematicians because individuals with good mathematical skills can earn more elsewhere. Fitz-Gibbon (1999) has also found some evidence that the take-up of mathematics A level might be higher in schools that are more effective at teaching the subject. If the quality of teaching is even more critical in mathematics than in other subjects, this would compound the relative pay problem.

Acknowledgement

Some of the work described in this chapter was conducted under a personal grant to Anna Vignoles from the ESRC, and this assistance is gratefully acknowledged.

Notes

1. The full research results summarized in this article can be found in Dolton and Vignoles (1999).
2. According to the Qualifications and Curriculum Agency (QCA), the proposed key skills course will cover a curriculum designed to develop Level 3 numeracy skills. This level is arguably equivalent to less than the middle tier of mathematics General Certificate of Secondary Education (GCSE).
3. See Chapter Four for a discussion about the inadequate preparation provided by the A level curriculum for some degree courses.
4. Dearing's report applied to the whole range of educational options available at 16–19, namely AS levels, A levels, General National Vocational Qualifications (GNVQs); BTEC Diplomas and NVQs, although this chapter focuses on the A level curriculum.
5. Dearing (1996: 32).
6. The wage premium from having A levels varies by gender and age (Dolton and Vignoles, 1997). For instance, the benefit of having A levels, in terms of pay, is higher at 33 than 23 (Dearden, Ferri and Meghir, 1998).
7. In 1858, the University of London introduced advanced, faculty-based matriculation examinations, the basis of today's A level system.
8. See, for example, Fogelman (1983).
9. In other words, taking A levels boosts your earnings, but the specific subjects studied make little difference.
10. Indeed, for women in this sample, mathematics A level had no statistically significant positive effect on earnings.
11. If the gap between mathematics GCSE and mathematics A level is much greater than the jump from mathematics O level to A level used to be, this might explain part of the decline in the numbers of students taking mathematics A level.
12. There have been a number of criticisms levelled at the methodology used in this research, however (Cresswell, 1996).
13. *Times Educational Supplement*, 26 August 1988.
14. It is possible that the ability tests used in our analysis measure a different type of intelligence from that actually used in the world of work. To the extent that this is the case, and that mathematics A level is a better measure of 'work intelligence', our efforts to allow separately for the effect of ability and mathematics A level on earnings will be undermined.
15. For an opposing view on this, and a discussion of the difficulties in making international comparisons in mathematics, see Brown (1998). Basic Skills Agency (1997) and Wolf and Steedman (1998) provide additional evidence.
16. In 1999, for example, just 59 per cent of 11 year olds reached the expected

standard in mathematics. The target is for 75 per cent of 11 year olds to reach this level by the year 2000, which appears ambitious, despite the numeracy hour and other initiatives.

17. Our research also looked at the effect of taking a broader curriculum. We found no evidence that taking a broader curriculum at A level necessarily increased earnings.

18. 'Teachers meeting the challenge of change', DfEE (1998c). These issues are also discussed in Chapter 1.

4 Disjunctions between School and University: The Case of Mathematics

Rosamund Sutherland

Graduate School of Education, University of Bristol

Introduction

The General Certificate of Secondary Education (GCSE) as a basis for higher education

Until the 1960s and 1970s school mathematics in the UK was driven by the needs of university mathematics. The Cockcroft Report[1] played an influential role in changing this top-down approach. With the advent of the new GCSE courses (1986) and the National Curriculum (1989) school mathematics became more grounded in what were perceived to be the needs of all young people.

Nowadays, many more students progress to university than was the case when the Cockcroft Report was being produced. Courses such as biological sciences and business studies draw increasingly on mathematics and mathematical modelling. Many students enter university to study such courses having only studied mathematics to GCSE level. Paradoxically, a school reform which emphasized understanding and problem solving is leaving students with such an inadequate background for dealing with the mathematical demands of their university courses that they often have to resort to rote learning of mathematics.

Effects of reduction in formal content at A level

The system is also unsatisfactory for many students who have studied A level mathematics. The following comment, made by a bright first-year engineering student at Bristol University who had been successful with school mathematics (obtaining a grade A at A level) illustrates the difficulties which many students have with the more abstract aspects of mathematics and mathematical modelling.

> It's easier to deal with numbers I find, than algebra … I don't know whether it lets me down … I think it's just because I haven't used it as much before … at school it's all numbers and you're just taught 'this is the right answer'… I'm a lot happier using numbers than I am using letters really. (Quoted in Barry and Sutherland, 1998)

Alice expresses her lack of familiarity with symbols and algebra. Her A level mathematics course does not appear to have enabled her to develop a sense of symbols (Arcavi, 1994) and mathematical structure, which is crucial for becoming an engineer.

> Even at a managerial level a good engineer requires deep numerate common-sense to grasp the essential structure of quantified data or argument … the engineer needs to be able to use algebra to analyse equations or expressions in a required context, e.g. to simplify in accordance with orders of magnitude of different terms. In being able to do this the engineer saves time and expense and very likely ensures the safety of any related process or procedure. A reduction in algebraic knowledge must lead to a reduction in the sharpness of professional focus. (Arcavi, 1994: 33)

Traditionally, school mathematics tended to present students with relatively abstract problem situations in which the more formal aspects of mathematics were emphasized. Reforms of the mathematics curriculum have resulted in a decreasing emphasis on these formal aspects[2] and an increasing emphasis on problem solving in realistic contexts, although unfortunately the notion of 'realistic' has often become contorted and trivialized (see, for example, Figures 4.4 and 4.5). A common-sense argument suggests that if mathematics education is to be both motivating and relevant, then young people should learn how to solve problems in realistic contexts. This is a sound argument. Unfortunately, the evidence from higher education suggests that an over-simplified application of this principle to the school curriculum has resulted in a generation of young people who have extreme difficulties in using mathematics at all, whatever the context.

The first part of this chapter examines the mathematical requirements of higher education courses, discussing the claim by universities that many undergraduates are not able to tackle difficult mathematics problems, work independently and use mathematics in applied situations. The second section provides some explanation for the disjunction between school and university mathematics, through examining the changes to the mathematics curriculum over the last 15 years. The chapter concludes with a plea for more attention to be paid to the complex relationship between teaching and learning mathematics in the school context. I would argue that if we are to avoid the massive experimentation with young people which results from rather dogmatic and evangelical-like curriculum reforms, characterized by the Cockcroft 'missionaries'[3] and the Numeracy Task Force, then we need to take a more considered and cautious approach to curriculum change.

The voice of higher education

Concerns about the mathematical backgrounds of undergraduates

University mathematicians and engineers have been relatively vociferous in expressing their concerns about the mathematical background of their undergraduates. In *Tackling the Mathematics Problem* (London Mathematical Society, 1995) university mathematicians identified three areas which are often problematic for mathematics undergraduates:

1. carrying out numerical and algebraic calculations with fluency and accuracy;
2. dealing with complex multi-step problems; and
3. using and understanding proof and associated deductive processes.

University engineers (Sutherland and Pozzi, 1995) have expressed similar views about the mathematical background of engineers, although their concern is more related to students' confidence and competence with mathematical modelling than with mathematical proof.

> Take for example modelling, there is a lot of talk about it now. Modelling used to be traditional applied mathematics, Newton's laws, statistics, dynamics and mechanics, properties of matter, e.g. looking at

> blocks on a plane and friction, that was modelling ... nowadays there
> is a lot of time spent on modelling at school by people who are not very
> rigorous and not able to see the end of the investigation. Where is the
> pay off?   (Quoted in Sutherland and Dewhurst, 1999)

Other university disciplines have received less attention, although degree
courses such as chemistry, computer science, earth sciences, biological
sciences and economics draw heavily on mathematics and mathematical
modelling. The issues are somewhat different for those courses which
require A level mathematics (e.g. mathematics, physics and the majority
of engineering courses) and those courses which usually only specify
GCSE mathematics as an entrance requirement (e.g. chemistry, biological
sciences, earth sciences and business studies). There are also different
issues facing departments which specify high entrance qualifications and
those which accept students with lower qualifications. Nevertheless there
is increasing evidence that across many subject disciplines there is a real
gap between what universities would ideally want students to know about
mathematics and what students come to university knowing. This gap
relates to the changing mathematical nature of school mathematics, the
variable mathematical experiences of undergraduates and the fact that
university departments are often not in a position to specify the mathematical qualifications which they would like students to have before they
enter university.

Mathematical requirements for entry to degree courses
Table 4.1 presents an overview of the mathematical requirements of a
range of different subject areas from particular university departments,
categorized according to the average point scores of undergraduates.[4]
This table highlights the variability in requirements within a particular
subject area. For example, some biological sciences departments require
mathematics grade C at A level and others require GCSE grade C.

The mathematical demands of particular undergraduate courses
We were told by university physicists from a department which requires
a grade A or B in A level mathematics that many students are shocked by

Table 4.1 *Specified mathematics requirements of university departments*

	Maths	Elec. Eng.	Mech. Eng.	Physics	Comp. Science	Biol. Science	Chem.	Econ.	Bus. Studies
Dept. A point score 21–30	A level grade A	A level grade B	A level grade A/B	A level grade B	GCSE grade not spec.	A level grade C	GCSE grade not spec.	A level grade B	GCSE grade A
Dept. B point score 11–20	A level grade C	A level grade E	A level grade C/D	A level grade A/B	A level maths/ or science grade E	GCSE grade C	GCSE grade C	GCSE grade C	GCSE grade C
Dept C point score 1–10	A level grade E	A level grade E	BTEC Nat. Dip	No infor- mation received	GCSE grade C	GCSE grade C	GCSE grade C	GCSE grade not spec.	GCSE grade C

Note: Classified with respect to the particular subject areas as: Dept A, point score of entrants 21–30; Dept B, point score of entrants 11–20; Dept C, point score of entrants 1–10.

the mathematical nature of their physics courses. These university physicists said that their students are no longer competent with such topics as basic algebra, use of exponentials, trigonometric functions, and differential and integral calculus. What can universities do about the situation? Physics departments around the country are closing. Will mathematics departments follow the same trend? Could school mathematics continue to exist if university mathematics disappeared?

Consider an example from an earth sciences course. This is a subject which has changed substantially over the last 20–30 years.

> Previously it was very much a descriptive subject, maybe more of an art, and it still has some of the features of being an art, for example being able to go into the field and see things. Now, at research level it is highly quantitative and very complex. The department here reflects the new style of geology by having people from the other fundamental sciences

who are applying the approach and skills of say physics, mathematics, chemistry, microbiology into the areas of geology and palaeontology.

Students do not expect courses related to geology to be so mathematical.

The students are very old-fashioned. They come to the University expecting a field science, whereas most of the ground breaking work carried out in geology is going to be at a theoretical or laboratory-based level. The subject now relies on people doing quite complex things in chemistry or laboratory-based biology or computer techniques or even analytical theory. There is virtually no difference between the complexities involved between modern geology research and physics. The students come with an expectation of a more descriptive science and are more resistant to the quantitative side. They are resistant to learning – they seem to want to leave the maths behind now. Maybe this is because geology can be entered at an amateur level when people are quite young, collecting gem stones, looking at dinosaurs in museums. It is similar to astrophysics – the difference between looking at comets and being prepared to do the activities that are happening today in research astro-physics.[5]

The geology department which teaches this earth sciences course has revised its undergraduate courses fundamentally to take into account the need to teach more mathematics to undergraduates. The mathematics course developed for earth sciences students includes such topics as units and dimensions, logarithms, exponential functions and algebra. Problem situations are always introduced in the context of earth sciences, as illustrated by the following example:

Consider a lake in which sediment is accumulating. If the sedimentation rate is approximately constant and compaction of sediments can be ignored then we might expect that the age of sediment at a given depth will be proportional to the age. A simple function describing such a relationship is: Age = k x Depth.

Differential prior mathematical attainment of undergraduates
Nevertheless the teaching demands are enormous. The modular degree structure means that students who are predominantly studying for an arts

degree may choose to study an earth sciences course. The mathematical background of an undergraduate on such a course could range from GCSE to a grade A in A level mathematics. For this subject there could not be a worse match between school and university mathematics.

Two factors are at play. Firstly, universities have generally down-graded their mathematical entry requirements. Mathematics and physics departments which would previously have required/preferred A level mathematics and further mathematics now accept the majority of students with only one A level in mathematics. Courses (e.g. chemistry) which might previously have required O level mathematics now accept students with a GCSE qualification, and there are many senses in which these are not equivalent examinations. Secondly, the mathematical demands of A level mathematics are becoming less rigorous. For example, in the case of algebra, the Royal Society (1997) report concluded that:

> Nowadays many students have to devote much valuable time to the development of algebraic and manipulative skills at the start of any A level course, and time throughout the course has to be found for students to work continuously on these algebraic activities.
>
> Many current A level examination questions provide students with more support with the algebraic aspects of a problem, or are less demanding algebraically than was the case 10–15 years ago.
>
> *(Teaching and Learning Algebra, Pre-19*: 23)

The discussion above highlights the essence of the problems faced by a range of university courses. As in the case of the earth sciences course, university courses which accept students with a high grade average are likely to have groups of students with a wide range of mathematical attainment from A level grade A to those with only GCSE mathematics. Market forces and modular degrees (which are associated with the market-place culture of pick-and-mix) mean that students cannot easily be 'told' to study optional mathematics courses at university. With such a potential difference in the mathematics background of undergraduates on a range of courses, it does not make sense to make A level type mathematics courses mandatory at university level.

Degree courses which accept a large proportion of students with lower A level grades and possibly only GCSE mathematics (see Table 4.1) have other problems to deal with. The general mathematics background of students studying science and engineering courses can be so weak that a wide range of fundamental mathematics topics has to be re-taught at university level. The resources are not often available to offer the sort of teaching and learning environments that these students need. Students can be expected to develop their mathematical knowledge through attending drop-in resource centres with an increasing reliance on computer-based learning. The evidence is that such provision does not meet the demands of these students. Reporting on the results of a diagnostic test given to engineering degree students, Croft says that:

> There are significant numbers of students who are weak across the whole spectrum of basic topics. Referring them to extra remedial material while their main maths course progresses is often the only option available, but it rarely seems to work. It takes a particularly highly motivated and mature student to do this. For the majority it is more appropriate to recommend a prolonged period on an alternative course at the right level, but this doesn't seem to happen. Engineering departments want students to be able to proceed with mainstream engineering courses alongside their well-prepared peers. Major problems are the mismatch between expectations and abilities and a failure to recognize what different levels of mathematical qualification really mean. This results in a tremendous amount of unhappiness and misery for the affected students, and puts teaching staff in a no-win situation.   (Croft, 1999)

Any provision which is viewed as remedial is quite understandably rejected by most students, who know that the lecturers who will be assessing them on their degree courses may be prejudiced by knowing about their mathematical weaknesses.

Nowadays there is a view that computers could perhaps do a better job than teachers, a convenient argument if an organization is trying to save money on human resources. This view is becoming more pervasive at both the school and university level and it relates to an implicit attempt to teacher-proof the curriculum. I will discuss later in this chapter why I believe that an increasing reliance on the use of computers for teaching basic mathematical ideas is unlikely to be effective.

Limitations of Advanced General National Vocational Qualifications (GNVQs) as a preparation for degree courses

Over the last few years advanced vocational qualifications have been recognized as an alternative option for post-16 students. Unfortunately for students who want to progress to study engineering and science degrees, the Advanced GNVQ qualifications do not adequately prepare them for the mathematical aspects of science and engineering degree courses. One of the reasons for this is that many students are accepted on Advanced GNVQ courses with a very weak background in mathematics. For example, in a recent survey of Advanced GNVQ Science courses which drew from seven further education colleges we found that just over half of the students were being accepted with a GCSE mathematics grade lower than C. We also found that many students made very little mathematical progression throughout the GNVQ course. The only mandatory mathematics course for Advanced GNVQ Science students is the core skill 'application of number' which is usually taught within the context of the science courses. We concluded that:

> The complex and embedded nature of mathematics within science makes it very unlikely that students themselves will pay attention to the appropriate mathematical aspects of a situation unless these are drawn to their attention by a teacher. However science teachers may find it difficult to pay attention to the mathematical aspects of a problem, as their attention will be on teaching the science. Our observations of the teaching of GNVQ science suggest that when teachers do notice that students might need to learn some mathematical ideas in order to progress with the science situation, they either provide 'little tips' for example 'work out area again, you'll get a really tiny number' or a stream of advice. When opportunities arose for discussion around a mathematical idea the constraint of time often meant that the teacher did not take time-out to work with the mathematics.   (Molyneux and Sutherland, 1996: 12)

How can universities respond to the changing mathematical backgrounds of undergraduates

In summary, it is not possible to make A level mathematics a requirement for a wide range of degree courses which actually need mathematics, because this would seriously affect student numbers. GCSE mathematics is an inadequate preparation for any degree course which has a quantitative component because:

1. the topics covered in GCSE are not treated in enough depth; and
2. knowledge of GCSE mathematics tends to atrophy in the years between GCSE and university education.

The mathematical component of Advanced GNVQ courses is also not an adequate preparation for many degree courses. University lecturers do not want to over-emphasize the mathematical requirements of their courses when students enter university because many students are anti-mathematics, despite the educational reforms which were aimed at making mathematics more friendly. One lecturer reported that, even when teaching with compassion and understanding of student difficulties, the lecturer can be told 'You can't expect me to be able to do this because I've only got a GCSE.'

Those outside the university system tend to think that universities, and in particular the higher ranking universities, have not been responsive to the changing mathematical background of undergraduates. On the contrary, their ongoing survival means that they have all had to change in various ways. Universities are attempting to deal with these problems by redesigning their first year courses, offering additional mathematics courses, providing drop-in workshops, small-group teaching and computer-based mathematics learning centres. A recent report on the challenges facing chemistry higher education (Mason, 1998) also draws attention to the range of preliminary courses that are provided for chemistry students to fill perceived gaps in numeracy. This report also emphasizes that the cost of extra provision often has to be met from declining resources.

Many departments are placing the 'difficult' areas of work (often mathematics) in optional courses or removing them altogether. In subjects such as biological sciences some of the most exciting new developments in the discipline occur at the intersection of biology and mathematics. Nowadays students may only be able to engage with these ideas if they choose to study for a research degree. So, at a time when the leading edge of a subject is relying more on mathematics, we have a situation where undergraduates are less able to experience and appreciate the intellectually challenging ideas in their chosen area of study.

There is also some suggestion that the mathematical background of undergraduates is influencing the quality of degrees, although universities are understandably cautious about discussing this issue. However, the four-year mathematics, engineering and physics degrees have developed partly as a response to the changing mathematical background of undergraduates.

Difficulties of studying basic mathematics during a degree course

It is not difficult to conclude that universities are not the best place for the majority of students to learn relatively fundamental mathematical ideas, which include both content and approaches to solving problems (the two being inseparable). It is unrealistic for universities to teach a completely disparate group of students the mathematics that are needed for a particular course. This would mean channelling more resources to the mathematically unprepared than to those better prepared, which would be inequitable, particularly at a time when funding per student is falling.

There is also some evidence from a study of engineering students (Barry and Sutherland, 1998) that undergraduates do not improve on subjects such as algebra as they progress through their degree courses, even when they are being supported by a range of extra classes. This is because topics like algebra are more effectively learned over a long period of time from a young age. In other words, school is the best time and place for the learning of such topics to take place.

University lecturers are not the best people to be teaching university students basic mathematics. Their energy should be directed at communicating the complex ideas of their discipline. Moreover, students do not expect to have to learn basic mathematics when they arrive at university.

Although I appreciate that the learning experiences of many undergraduates could be improved vastly, I would like to emphasize that this is a separate issue from the one of adequately preparing students in mathematics before they enter university. In other words, we should have a national system in which students learn what in most countries would be considered to be pre-university mathematics before they go to university.

It is clearly inefficient for universities to be attempting to teach students with such wide-ranging mathematical backgrounds and they do not have, and are not being given, the resources to do so. In such a situation the quality of degrees must be being eroded, because the time spent studying basic mathematics at university is not being spent on the subjects which students come to university to study.

Unintended effects of reforms

Evaluating curriculum change in school mathematics
In the 1980s the reforms to the mathematics curriculum paid attention to the needs of everyday life and employment. As discussed already, problem solving and the application of mathematics were emphasized:

> All children need experience of applying the mathematics they are learning both to familiar everyday situation and also to the solution of problems which are not exact repetitions of exercises which have already been practised. (Cockcroft, 1982: para. 321)

Changes were made to the whole system. The National Curriculum was implemented, and text books and assessment approaches were all transformed with the expectation that young people would become more successful at using mathematics in a range of situations, both outside school and in other 'school' subjects.

Formal and informal methods
In this section I will examine why the reforms based on the recommendations of the Cockcroft Report do not appear to have resulted in the desired outcomes. The various strands of the recommendations all centre

around the idea of making mathematics more meaningful for the majority. Influenced by research of the day, there was a big push to encourage teachers to value the knowledge children bring to the classroom and thus draw on their informal methods.

> In algebra and in the other topics investigated, the research has found that children frequently tackle mathematics problems with methods that have little or nothing to do with what has been taught. This may be because mathematics teaching is often seen as an initiation into rules and procedures which, though very powerful (and therefore attractive to teachers), are often seen by children as meaningless. It follows that children's methods and their levels of understanding need to be taken far more into account, however difficult this may be in practice.
>
> (Küchemann, 1981: 118)

The argument for taking more account of children's methods relates to the conclusion that children 'frequently tackle mathematics problems with methods that have little or nothing to do with what has been taught'. I have argued elsewhere that a view that children's mathematical methods in school have little to do with what has been taught is misconceived (Sutherland, 1998). Detailed analysis of the reason a student might give for solving a problem in a particular way almost always reveals a reason which makes sense to the student and which somehow relates to previous teaching. So when 15-year-old Eloise says that *a* stands for 1 and *b* stands for 2, it could be concluded that what she had learned did not bear any relationship to what was taught. But when questioned, she revealed that her conceptions did relate to her primary school practices 'when we were little we used to do a code like that ... in junior school ... A would equal 1, B equals 2, C equals 3 ... there were possibilities of A being 5 and B being 10 and that lot ... but it would come up too high a number to do it ... it was always in some order'.[6]

The case of 'trial and improvement'
The relationship between formal and informal methods has become complex because informal methods have sometimes become the taught and

thus institutionalized method. Take, for example, trial and improvement methods for solving equations as illustrated in Figure 4.1. This is the sort of approach which a pupil is likely to use spontaneously when presented for the first time with an equation to solve, and it is also a sensible approach to solving very simple equations. Yet, this informal approach has become a 'taught' and examined method (Figure 4.2). Nowadays there is increasing evidence that young people routinely use a trial and improvement approach to solving equations in situations where it is neither effective nor efficient, as illustrated by the second example in Figure 4.2.

> It is a widely held view that trial and improvement is somehow natural and spontaneous. However, we believe that this method has become taught and examined to such an extent that for many pupils it is the 'official school method'. (Royal Society, 1997: 29)

Figure 4.1 *Trial and improvement – GCSE examination question*

---

17 **The equation $x^2 - x - 1 = 0$ has a solution between 1 and 2. Use trial and improvement to find this solution correct to 2 decimal places.**

You must show all your trials

Figure 4.2 *Trial and improvement – secondary school pupil methods*

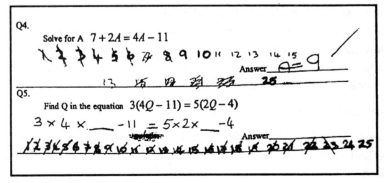

Source: Vile, 1996.

Interviews with 16–19 year old vocational students indicate that their approaches to converting between units within the context of science can be characterized by the 'trial and improvement' methods which have become prioritized at school (Molyneux and Sutherland, 1996). This involves trying a range of conversion factors and either multiplying or dividing until the answer 'looks right', and can be a very inefficient approach in the context of scientific practice. Whereas traditional schooling often led to an inappropriate use of formal mathematical methods in problem-solving situations, nowadays schooling is leading to an inappropriate use of 'informal' methods. What is being forgotten is the notion that some mathematical methods may be more appropriate or efficacious then others in particular problem-solving situations. Emphasizing the process of 'using and applying mathematics' may have been the intention of the reforms, but the introduction of league tables and Key Stage tests has led teachers to encourage their pupils to produce correct answers, whatever the method.

Effects of curriculum reform on primary school mathematics
An analysis of one of the most popular UK primary mathematics textbooks reveals an almost recipe-like interpretation of the Cockcroft recommendations (Figure 4.3). This can be summarized in the following way. When teaching a new topic:

1. present pupils with a realistic situation;
2. ask pupils to work in groups and estimate the computation;
3. ask each child to find his/her own way to calculate the exact answer; and
4. check the answer with a calculator.

What can be noted from this example is that:

1. what is called 'estimation' is prioritized over computation, but in effect it is likely that it is 'guessing' which is being encouraged; and
2. informal methods seem to be prioritized over algorithmic methods.

Figure 4.3 *Teaching multiplication – excerpt from the teacher's guide to one of the most popular schemes in the UK*

B **Multiplying and dividing by one- and two-digit numbers** **G** **I**

Part 1: Multiplying by one- and two-digit numbers

1 Display several items each costing up to £10.

70p   £3·05   £7·50   £9·99

2 Ask the children, working in twos or threes, to agree on and write down an estimate/approximation for the total cost, if eight of each item were bought. Compare their results.

Eight of the paperback books, worth £3·05 each, would cost just over £24 because ...

You would pay about £100 for 10 compact discs at £9·99 each because ...

STEPS 5

Resources

School
Facsimile notes and coins; calculators

Scheme
Book 5(2), pages 56 and 57

In this activity, the children are encouraged to transfer their knowledge of multiplying whole numbers to multiplying decimal numbers. The most important factor is that the children have a strategy for solving problems from previous experience.

3 Ask each child to find his/her own way to calculate the exact answers, using pencil-and-paper methods, and then to check the answers with a calculator.

4 Discuss the range of methods used, including the standard algorithm (shown here last), if appropriate.

£3·25 × 8
↓

a.
£3·00 × 8 = £24·00
20p × 8 = £ 1·60
5p × 8 = £ 0·40
£3·25 × 8 = £26·00

b.
```
  325
 × 8
2600
  24
```
→
```
£3·25
  ×8
£26·00
```

c.
```
£3·25
  ×8
£26·00
   2
```

5 Repeat for examples requiring multiplication of an amount up to £10 by a two-digit number, e.g. £3·57 × 23 and demonstrate some of the methods chosen.

a.
£3 × 23 = £69·00
50p × 23 = £ 11·50
7p × 23 = £ 1·61
£3·57 × 23 = £82·11

b.
```
  357
 × 23
 7140
+1071
 8211
```
→
```
£3·57
 ×23
£82·11
```

c.
```
£3·57
 × 23
£10·71  (£3·57×3)
£71·40  (£3·57×20)
£82·11
   1
```

Examples b and c highlight the importance of estimating/approximating answers to know where to plot the decimal point so that the answer is sensible.

Source: STEPS Mathematics (1997), London: Collins Educational.

I am not arguing that informal methods do not have a role, but rather that a reform which presents new teaching practices in a dogmatic way without offering intelligent explanations for these approaches is doomed to failure from the point of view of learning mathematics.

Confusing applications and pseudo-practical approaches

A concern with problem solving has led to the placing of mathematics in the most contorted and contrived of problem situations which could be distracting to all those but the most confident from learning mathematics. I realize that textbooks are only one way of presenting mathematics to pupils, but during the 1980s and 1990s very many pupils in the UK were learning mathematics from individualized textbook schemes. An analysis of these texts suggests that pupils might have difficulty making sense of the mathematical ideas which they are supposed to be learning both at secondary level (see, for example, Figure 4.4) and at a primary level (see, for example, Figure 4.5).[7]

Another related reason why the more formal aspects of mathematics, including algebra, have become so under-emphasized in the UK relates to changes in teaching approaches. Individualized mathematics schemes (e.g. School Mathematics Independent Learning Experience (SMILE)) were implicitly motivated by a desire to communicate to teachers that their teaching would be more effective if it focused on individuals, moving away from whole-class teaching. This was based on sound reasons related to children taking more responsibility for their learning, but nevertheless the 'hidden message' was that teaching the whole class was ideologically unsound. This shift in teaching approach, away from the teacher towards individual and group work, made it difficult to teach mathematics which pupils were unlikely to invent for themselves through problem-solving activity. This includes algebra, trigonometry, geometry and proof. Nowadays, as I shall discuss later in this chapter, whole-class teaching is being re-emphasized through the National Numeracy Strategy.

To summarize, in the 1980s and early 1990s changes to school mathematics were influenced by a number of interrelated factors which included a view that: learning does not relate to what the teacher teaches; students learn more effectively if the curriculum is individualized; students will learn more effectively if the teacher draws on their informal methods; informal methods are as effective as more formal methods for solving problems. Each one of these principles could be related to a more complex theory which makes sense as a whole, but, used in practice separated from any theoretical guidelines, they result in a nonsense approach to mathematics education.

Figure 4.4 *A pseudo-practical approach to teaching the equivalence of algebraic expressions*

A **Expressions**

The manager of a supermarket has to check the stock at the end of each week.

A1 At the beginning of a week there were 740 cans of Fizi-Cola in the supermarket.

During the week 230 cans were delivered to the supermarket, and 410 cans were sold.

How many cans were there in the supermarket at the end of the week?

A2 At the start of a week in a hot summer there were 3800 cans in stock.
1200 were delivered during the week and 1700 were sold.

How many cans were there at the end of the week?

Figure 4.4 *A pseudo-practical approach to teaching the equivalence of algebraic expressions* contd

Every week the manager has to do the same kind of calculation.

He starts with the number at the beginning of the week.

He adds on the number delivered.

He subtracts the number sold.

The numbers change from week to week. They are **variable**. But he does the same kind of calculation with them every time.

We can use letters to stand for numbers which vary.

Let *b* stand for the number at the beginning of a week.
Let *d* stand for the number delivered to the supermarket.
Let *s* stand for the number sold.

The manager does the calculation *b + d − s.*

A calculation with letters standing for numbers is called an **expression**. The expression *b + d − s* is the number of cans in stock at the end of a week.

A3   (a)   Does the manager get the same result if he
            starts with the number at the beginning of a week.
            then subtracts the number sold, then adds the number delivered?
      (b)   Write the expresseion for this.

Figure 4.4 *A pseudo-practical approach to teaching the equivalence of algebraic expressions* contd

A4 Which of these expressions also give the number
    at the end of a week?
    (a) d - s + b   (b) b - s + d   (c) d - s - b
    (d) d - b - s   (e) s - d - b   (f) b + s - d

EQUIVALENT EXPRESSIONS

The expressions   and
always give the same result.
no matter what numbers b.d.s stand for.
They are called equivalent expressions.

A5 Write down as many other expressions as you can which are
    equivalent to b + d - s.

A6 Rajesh is given some money at the beginning of the day.
    He spends some on sweets, some on comics, and some on bus fares.

    Let g stand for the amount he is given, in pence.
    Let s stand for the amount he spends on sweets.
    Let c stand for the amount he spends on comics.
    Let f stand for the amount he spends on fares.

    (a) Write down an expression for the number of pence he has left.
    (b) Now write down an many other expressions as you can which are
        equivalent to the first one.

Source: Royal Society (1997), *Teaching and Learning Algebra pre-19*. Report of a
Royal Society/Joint Mathematical Council Working Group. London: Royal
Society.

Figure 4.5 *A pseudo-practical approach to the teaching of subtraction*

(a) Two of the numbers have a difference of 11.
Write these numbers.
(b) Write a pair of numbers with a difference of 7.
(c) Find other pairs with a difference of 7.

Source: Howson, Harries and Sutherland (1999), *Primary School Mathematics Textbooks: An international study summary.* London: Qualifications and Curriculum Authority.

Reforms to school algebra

In order to illustrate some of these points, I will now consider the case of algebra in more detail. As reflected in new textbook schemes and examination questions, school algebra in the UK began to focus on generalizing from patterns. The emphasis was on generalizing in natural language with the algebraic language being introduced at a later stage in the activity. Expression of a generalization in the English language was viewed as more 'natural' than a generalization in algebra. The difficulty with this approach is that the algebraic language is usually a more effective medium for generalizing in mathematics than natural language. Many pupils are not aware of the mathematical game they are playing and so, when solving 'generalizing' problems (e.g. Figure 4.6), produce valid but mathematically inappropriate descriptions such as 'you can get four matches in one box and in two you can get seven' as opposed to a generalization such as 'the number of matches is three multiplied by the number of squares plus one'. The subtle issue here is that these types of problems *are* intended for pupils to learn algebra. However, if pupils are not aware of this 'algebra game' they will produce solutions which cannot be easily 'translated' into an algebraic expression such as $M = 3S + 1$.

This move away from using symbols was influenced by research evidence which showed that the majority of pupils were not interpreting literal symbols in ways which were appropriate to algebra (Booth, 1984; Kieran, 1989; Küchemann, 1981).

> These results resonated with schoolteachers who had always found that school algebra alienated many of their pupils. In the UK, greatly influenced by this research, there began to be a shift in what constituted school algebra in the pre-16 curriculum with a substantial move away from the use of literal symbols. In the UK the Cockcroft Report also had a considerable influence on changes to school mathematics and, in particular, school algebra. Recommendations related to 'understanding', situating mathematics within 'practical' problems and the need for a differentiated curriculum have all influenced the curriculum in ways which have resulted in less emphasis being placed on algebra.
>
> (Royal Society, 1997: 3)

Figure 4.6 *Generalising from patterns of squares*

2 a) Complete the mapping diagram by looking for a pattern in the squares.

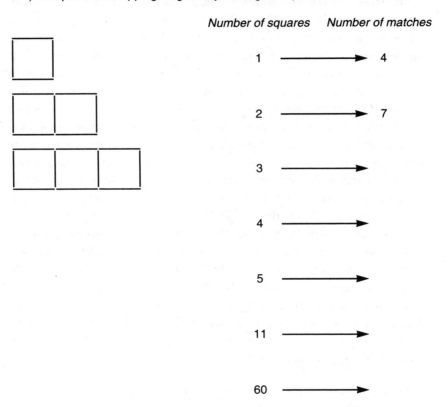

b) Write down a rule which explains how you got the second number from the first.

c) If possible write down the **rule** in algebra.

Much of classical school algebra had involved teaching standard algorithms for solving equations. These standard algorithms have become associated with traditional and rote ways of teaching which have been perceived as being in opposition to relevance and understanding. In this respect, rote learning methods have been replaced by informal context-specific activities which may not relate to algebraic development. The unintended effects of this celebrating of relevance has been that the majority of pupils pre-16 have had very little experience of symbolic algebra. For many students this is not always redressed at the post-16 level, even if students study A level mathematics. Our study with engineering undergraduates (Barry and Sutherland, 1999) suggests that it is only those students who have studied further mathematics at A level who are confident enough with algebra before they enter university engineering courses. This is manifestly inequitable as many schools no longer offer A level further mathematics.

When faced with the more formal mathematics which is an inherent part of the quantitative aspects of higher degree courses, students at university become alienated, give up, memorize what they need to know, or find other resources to help them with their mathematics.

> Well my girlfriend understands maths, thankfully, and I've been crying to her most of the time.   (Quoted in Barry and Sutherland, 1999)

Approaches to curriculum reform
To conclude this section, my argument is that recommendations in the Cockcroft Report (many of them influenced by research) have been too 'dogmatically' translated into curriculum reforms. The current changes in the form of the National Numeracy Strategy suggest that this approach to curriculum reform is still the dominant practice. Is a more 'humble' and critical approach possible within a massive education system?

Teaching and learning mathematics

Bruner expresses very well the issue which I have been struggling with for some time:

Now to pedagogy. Early on, children encounter the hoary distinction between what is known by 'us' (friends, parents, teachers, and so on) and what in some larger sense is simply 'known'. In these post-positivist, perhaps 'post-modern' times, we recognize all too well that the 'known' is neither God-given truth nor, as it were, written irrevocably in the Book of Nature. Knowledge in this dispensation is always putatively revisable. But revisability is not to be confused with free-for-all relativism, the view that since no theory is the ultimate truth, all theories, like all people, are equal. We surely recognize the distinction between Popper's 'World-Two' of personally held beliefs, hunches, and opinions and his 'World Three' of justified knowledge. But what makes the latter 'objective' is not that it constitutes some positivist's free-standing, aboriginal reality, but rather that it has stood up to sustained scrutiny and been tested by the best available evidence.   (Bruner, 1996: 61)

Paying attention to the social and cultural aspects of mathematics and mathematics learning does not imply a belief in an absolute body of mathematical knowledge, nor does it imply returning to traditional curricula and traditional teaching approaches. Rather it implies critically examining the mathematics and associated symbol systems which we want pupils to learn. It foregrounds the role of representing ideas, on paper or in computers. It also foregrounds the social and historical aspects of learning.

Mathematics before pedagogy
One explanation for the reason why the Cockcroft reforms did not have the desired and intended effects is that those responsible for driving the reforms did not understand the point made by Bruner in the above quote. They appear to have believed that *all* approaches to solving mathematical problems are equal. Another explanation relates to a dominant pedagogical approach which draws on pupils' own approaches and has no mechanism for confronting them with ways of judging which methods are more or less efficient in which situations. I am not sure whether those who have recently been pushing interactive whole-class teaching approaches (e.g. Reynolds and Muijs, 1999) appreciate that one of the

characteristics of many Pacific Rim and Continental European mathematics classrooms is an explicit discussion, organized by the teacher, and often centring around pupils' productions on the board, of the efficiency of different (yet all correct) methods of solving a problem. There is a real danger in focusing on 'pedagogy' or teaching methods in isolation from an analysis of the mathematics to be learned. It leads to a reification of methods, such as individualized learning, group work and interactive teaching as opposed to an unpacking of the complexity of teaching and learning mathematics.

In some senses it is an over-simplified focus on pedagogy, or teaching method, which has led to a strange interpretation of 'realistic' in the school mathematics context. 'Pupils learn better if mathematics is related to their everyday experiences' becomes a mantra which appears to be used almost unthinkingly (at least from the point of view of learning mathematics) by those who write textbooks and those who write examinations and assessment items. In the UK many of those who influence what children learn in schools do not seem to be very good at 'unpacking' complexity. It could be argued of course that the pace of curriculum reforms such as the National Curriculum, GCSE and now the National Numeracy Strategy does not give anyone time to analyse complexity. In other words, the pace of change pushes in the direction of over-simplification and dogma.

The case of mental mathematics and the place of algorithms

Take the current polarization of 'mental' mathematics and work on paper. Now paper-based algorithms have evolved because they do some of the work for us. They are valuable because we can use them without thinking too much about them. A scientist when faced with an embedded conversion problem within his or her scientific practices would not want to take time out to 'understand' the method he or she is using from a mathematical perspective. A scientist needs, almost unthinkingly, to be able to carry out the procedure of conversion and to focus on the scientific situation. In other words, he or she needs an algorithmic method of conversion because it can provide an effective structure for converting which should free the mind in order to pay attention to the more salient aspects of the situation.

If I want, for example, to carry out the computation 394 x 47, I could possibly manipulate the numbers in my head, using such notions as 47 is three less than 50, but I know that I personally cannot rely on purely mental approaches except within simple multiplication problems. If I set out the problem as:

$$\begin{array}{r} 394 \\ \times\ 47 \\ \hline \\ \hline \end{array}$$

and follow the algorithmic approach, there is a built-in system for me to follow. The way of setting out on paper and the rules which need to be followed support me to produce a correct answer. Of course, I should understand how the method works but I will only need to interrogate this understanding if something untoward happens when I am carrying out the process. Wertsch argues that when asked who carried out the problem the answer should be 'I and the cultural tool I employed did' (Wertsch, 1998: 29). This notion of the potential and power of cultural tools is almost completely missing from curriculum documents, textbooks and the mathematics education culture in the UK.

Although I may ultimately want to use an algorithmic approach in a 'relatively' mechanistic way, this does not imply that the teaching of multiplication should take a mechanistic approach. Teaching should help children understand that there are many ways of solving the same mathematics problem and that, depending on the circumstances, some methods are more efficient than others. Teachers are not being helped to understand this complexity if they are being more or less told how to teach, which interestingly was the case with the 'Cockcroft' missionaries and is the case with the National Numeracy Strategy. In both cases it seems that there is an implicit view that teachers are almost the cause of pupils' difficulties and that we can somehow teacher-proof the curriculum if we make their work as rule-abiding as possible.

Individualized computer-based learning systems

Another manifestation of a teacher-proofing of the curriculum is individualized learning. Whereas the textbook form of individualization is now becoming out of favour, the computer-based form is increasingly being pushed by computer manufacturers. I suggest that this individualized approach is flawed for two reasons. The first is from a theoretical position that says that the human is a crucial mediator of mathematical knowledge. It is only the human teacher who can engage in the sort of messy dialogue which is necessary for the progression of a complex knowledge domain such as mathematics. Schooling is about providing all pupils with access to the mathematical knowledge that has developed over centuries. The process of communicating this knowledge to pupils cannot be through formalized computer-aided learning systems, because computers (at least at present) are just not able to do this sort of work. The second reason why I argue against the pervasive introduction of individualized computer-based learning systems is that their introduction will result in a deskilling of teachers. Given my belief in the quality of the 'thinking' teacher, I consider this potential dumbing-down of teachers to be near disastrous in terms of the education of future generations.

Conclusion

More and more young people in the UK are progressing to university. The disjunction between school mathematics and the mathematical demands of a wide range of university courses is increasingly becoming a barrier to the progress of knowledge. Here I mean both knowledge as an individual construct and knowledge as a social construct. I wonder if the educationalists and policy-makers who were responsible for driving forward reforms such as GCSE and GNVQ paid attention to the need for a planned mathematical match between school and higher education. Or has a preoccupation with just-in-time learning motivated a view that students will be able to learn what they need when they need it? The evidence from higher education is that this is not the case.

Unfortunately, learning mathematics is a complex and messy process, a process which takes time and which cannot be reduced to a robot-like focus on transmitting bits of knowledge. Learning mathematics requires an educational system which supports and does not inhibit good teaching, an educational system which tries to understand the theories behind the reforms that it imposes on teachers and is honest about what is known and what is not yet known about teaching and learning mathematics in the classroom.

In the case of mathematics, theoretical knowledge has developed over centuries. In the case of teaching and learning mathematics, we are on much more shaky theoretical grounds. Although my work is influenced by a particular sociocultural approach to teaching and learning (Bruner, 1996; Wertsch, 1998), I also believe that this theoretical approach needs long-term evaluation and development in classroom situations. In other words, we do not yet know enough to be dogmatic about teaching and learning. But we do know enough to provide reasoned explanations for curriculum reforms which draw to a certain extent on theoretical ideas. It is my experience that teachers want to engage with these explanations.

So, whereas I have argued against the pervasive use of 'trial and improvement' for solving mathematics problems, I am now going to argue for a 'trial and improvement' approach to teaching and learning. In this approach the teacher modifies what he or she does in response to feedback on pupils' learning. In this approach teachers are thinking individuals who have themselves been educated in a national system which emphasizes challenge and explanation. It would seem that a national system which is encouraging more and more young people to study in higher education could meet this criteria. However, I am not optimistic about this possibility if knowledge is reduced to bits and bytes of information which can be delivered just-in-time by unintelligent computers.

Notes

1. *Mathematics Counts* (1982), Report on the Committee of Inquiry into the Teaching of Mathematics in Schools, London: HMSO.
2. For a further discussion of this issue, see *Teaching and Learning Algebra pre-19*, Report by The Royal Society/Joint Mathematical Council of the UK (1997).
3. 'DES-funded advisory teachers, both primary and secondary, appointed in each LEA to spread their own good practice by working mainly in classrooms alongside other teachers' (Brown, 1996: 7).
4. These results are taken from a recently conducted study on the mathematical knowledge expected of undergraduates across a wide range of disciplines (Sutherland and Dewhurst, 1999).
5. This interview was carried out as part of the project Mathematics Education: Framework for Progression from 16–19 to HE (Sutherland and Dewhurst, 1999).
6. Taken from the results of the ESRC 'Project AnA – the Gap between Arithmetical and Algebraic Thinking' and written about in more detail in Sutherland (1995).
7. This example was taken from a recent study which compared primary mathematics textbooks from five different countries (Harries and Sutherland, 1999).

5 Mathematics for Some or Mathematics for All? Curious UK Practices in International Context

Alison Wolf
Mathematical Sciences Group, Institute of Education, University of London

Introduction

It is notoriously difficult for a fish to notice the water around it; and almost as hard, it seems, to see one's own national education system as anything but the natural order of things. Presumably because everyone experienced their own system during childhood, it acquires a taken-for-granted, timeless quality. This in turn makes it extraordinarily difficult for politicians, journalists, education professionals and parents to recognize that unquestioned practices are both unusual, and, in principle, changeable.

This is certainly and unfortunately true for mathematics. This chapter places school mathematics for 14 to 19 year olds in comparative perspective, and describes how unique and how peculiar England and Wales (and to a lesser extent Scotland) are in their approach. Moreover, while this may be a familiar fact among scholars of comparative education, it is not, in my experience, well known even to university specialists in mathematics education, let alone maths teachers, civil servants, politicians or the media.

The first part of this chapter summarizes the current approach to upper secondary mathematics education in UK schools, and identifies some of the major ways in which it is distinctive, not to say highly unusual. The second and third sections provide a more in-depth discussion of how our approach compares with that of other countries, providing an international context first for academic and then for vocational programmes. The fourth and final section asks who is out of step – the British or the rest of the world? Its conclusion is that our current approach does not and will not produce high standards of mathematics attainment among British (and, again, especially English) young people, and that economic trends make such high standards increasingly and urgently desirable.

Where we are (and some of the ways in which we got here)

As Chapter One explained, maths is a more or less universal part of every British young person's education up to the end of compulsory schooling, and the vast majority – about 91 per cent – obtain some sort of certification in mathematics at or around the age of 16, typically a General Certificate of Secondary Education (GCSE) or a Standard Grade pass in mathematics, obtained through a public examination (Wolf and Steedman, 1998). However, the standard reached by many of these 16 year olds is modest. Only 47 per cent of GCSE entrants, or approximately 43 per cent of the age cohort (1998 figures) obtain a C grade or above, i.e. a grade deemed equivalent to the old O level and as such commonly referred to, at least among the realistic young, as a 'pass'.

The effects of 'tiered' GCSE entry
Not all the candidates for GCSE mathematics have followed the same syllabus: nor, for most of the grades awarded, have all those with a given result. The GCSE in mathematics is for the most part offered on the basis of three distinct 'tiered' syllabuses,[1] covering different amounts of material, but with overlapping grades. Thus, a candidate for the lower tier can obtain grades that range from a D to a G; an intermediate tier candidate can get anything from a B to an E; and an upper tier candidate can obtain grades between A* and C. (All candidates can also end up with an 'Ungraded' or fail grade.) Scottish candidates similarly are entered for one of three distinct Standard Grade examinations (Foundation, General or Credit).

The existence of several different maths syllabuses means that schools have to make decisions about which maths course students should be encouraged or allowed to follow. While many countries operate with more than one maths syllabus in the middle and upper years of secondary schooling, the system of tiering combined with public examinations and overlapping grades is not merely unusual but unique. In addition, the advent of league tables has created pressures on school decision-making which are proving catastrophic for the teaching of maths in English and Welsh schools.

Schools are judged by the proportions of their pupils who receive A–C grades in their GCSEs. There have been worries expressed for some time that, among other things, this leads to an emphasis on the marginal C/D grade pupils and relative neglect of others, especially the lowest achieving. However, the most dramatic evidence of the effect of league tables, through the incentives they create, can be observed in GCSE mathematics.

Until 1993, the highest grade that could be obtained by a pupil taking the Intermediate papers was a C. To obtain a B (or A) the Higher tier was necessary. While a C was moderately desirable from a league table point of view, a grade distribution in which it was the top mark was fairly obviously undesirable to parents and made it quite clear to them (and to students) that this was very much a scaled down syllabus. However, in 1994, a B grade became available for Intermediate candidates. That is, students following the Intermediate syllabus and taking the Intermediate papers could obtain a B as well as a C. Only for an A or A* grade is the upper tier syllabus now necessary.

The effects were immediate and dramatic. In 1993, 28.5 per cent of GCSE maths entries were for the Higher tier. In 1994, one year later, the figure was 16.5 per cent, where it has pretty much remained.[2] In other words, *the proportion of students taking this upper tier GCSE has been almost halved in the recent past.* As a proportion of the age cohort, moreover, the figures are lower still, as about nine per cent of 16 year olds do not sit for mathematics GCSE at all. In 1985, on the eve of the GCSE's introduction, 24 per cent of the age cohort passed O level mathematics, with a syllabus which included mathematics equivalent to (and in some respects more advanced than) the content of the GCSE higher tier. In other words, the proportion of 16 year olds reaching a moderately advanced level of mathematics at the end of their compulsory schooling is now significantly lower than it was 15 years ago.[3]

The combination of tiering with league table pressures is, as we have noted, unique to this country. However, what is really unusual is that, for the vast majority of English and Welsh students, Intermediate or Lower tier mathematics GCSE, taken at age 16, comprises their last exposure to a formal examined mathematics course. It is the last, because, at age 16, most move onto either a small number of A levels, or a single subject full-time vocational course such as a General National Vocational Qualification (GNVQ) or a Business and Technician Education Council (BTEC) National Diploma. (See page 122 for a fuller discussion of these awards.) As we discuss in the following sections, this makes them very different from their overseas contemporaries in both the length of their mathematical studies and in the total content they cover. It also has enormous implications for their own access to later subjects of study.

Mathematics GCSE plays a critical role in deciding which course of study a young person will follow post-16. Most institutions specify five or more GCSEs at C or above, including mathematics and English, as the prerequisite for A level studies; and data on young people's careers bear out that this is indeed generally the case. Both English and mathematics are taken by the vast majority of the cohort, and English, with 57 per cent of passes at C or above, appears somewhat 'easier' than mathematics, for which the figure is 47 per cent.[4] More significantly, very few candidates with a C in mathematics do not also get a C in English. Maths grades thus have become in practice the single most critical determinant of whether an individual will take A levels or follow another course post-16 (Further Education Unit, 1994).

Increased numbers in upper secondary education

The numbers of young people taking A levels, or, in Scotland, Highers, have increased enormously in recent years, both absolutely and as a proportion of the age cohort. In this the British are following, somewhat belatedly, a general trend in the developed world towards near-universal participation in full-time upper secondary education, whether academic or largely vocational (Green, Wolf and Leney, 1999). By summer 1999, 36 per cent (over one-third) of English 16–17 year olds were enrolled for A levels, a further 35 per cent were in other full-time programmes, and another 15 per cent were receiving part-time education or training, often through a formal apprenticeship or participation in a government training scheme. The following two sections describe what this means in terms of the post-GCSE mathematics education currently provided to our young people, and the contrast between UK practice and that of other countries.

Mathematics for academic track pupils

Diversity of A and AS levels
As the numbers taking A level have increased, so too have the number of subjects offered: to physics, English, French have been added business studies, photography and sports studies. What has not changed, however, is the extraordinary degree of specialization characteristic of the English, Welsh and Northern Irish system. Students are free to select any combination of subjects which schools or colleges can offer, and in principle can sit for as many subjects as they please. In practice, however, the modal number remains three, and these three subjects occupy anything from the vast bulk to the whole of the typical academic sixth former's study programme. Government attempts to broaden sixth-form studies through the original AS level – half the content, the same difficulty as an A level – failed. I return below to the question of whether current AS/A level reforms will be more effective.

Decline of mathematics A level
Chapter One has already described briefly the history of A level mathematics entries. It is one of general, although uneven, decline from the peak of the late 1950s and early 1960s, when one A level pass in six was in mathematics, to the one in ten of today. However, from the point of view of both national economic interest and individual opportunity, the absolute number of A level passes on mathematics is the more important. As Table 5.1 shows,[5] we have reached a situation where the absolute

number of A level passes in mathematics is substantially lower than in the 1980s or even the 1970s. In other words, at a time when the absolute demand for mathematics skills is higher than ever before in both the economy and in academic life, supply is actually falling.

Table 5.1 *Mathematics A levels: absolute number of entries, and entries as a percentage of total A level entries (summer and winter)*

	No.	As % of all A level entries	No. of A level entries
1955 (summer only)	21,467	15.6	137,867
1959 (summer only)	31,970	17.3	184,558
1964	56,867	16.8	338,608
1969	65,826	13.6	482,325
1974	65,841	13.1	501,289
1979	79,412	14.3	554,941
1984	90,688	14.4	627,599
1992	66,395	9.9	669,584
1994	60,419	8.9	675,572
1997	63,858	8.9	713,569
1998	64,346	8.9	724,852

Note: For 17-year-old entrants, the figures for maths entries as a proportion of the total are virtually identical to those for the whole population.
Source: DES/DfEE School Examination Statistics (annual).

This does not mean that young people of the sort who used to take mathematics A level are now rejecting it. On the contrary, in relation to the size of the population of 18 year olds, take-up has been quite stable in recent years. Instead what has happened is that the huge overall expansion of A levels has not been reflected in mathematics entries. The 'new' expanded A level population is taking quite different subjects, as Figure 5.1 demonstrates. With low birthrates in the UK, as indeed is the case throughout the Western world, we cannot rely on cohort size to provide a larger mathematically competent population.

Figure 5.1 *Mathematics A level entries and total A level entries in relation to cohort size, 1955–1998*

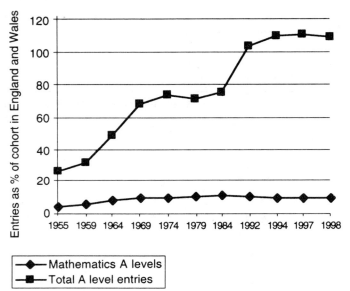

Note: A level figures are all entries and not just 18-year-olds. Average number of entries per student is around three: so dividing the total entries by a little over three gives an approximation of the proportion of 18-year-olds taking A levels.

Source: DES/DfEE School Examinations Statistics (annual).

AS levels

One attempt to increase take-up of mathematics was through AS levels, which were first set in 1989 and designed as a way of broadening the sixth-form syllabus, and encouraging academic track students to take a wider range of subjects. Their architects were especially keen that science students should take an arts subject and vice-versa. Take-up, however, was very low. This is partly because of timetabling and resourcing problems, and partly because it soon became generally accepted that, while an AS level might only cover half the content of an A level, two of the original (pre-2000) AS levels were much harder to pass than one A level. Within the AS grouping, mathematics has actually been the greatest success in terms of candidate numbers, with only general studies coming anywhere near its total entry. However, it is also the curriculum subject in which it has been quite common to enter A level candidates for AS as well (especially before modular A levels became standard). Unusually for old-style (pre-2000) AS levels, many candidates were reported by teachers (and institutions) to be either 'downscaling' from a full A level, or taking the AS as a dry run for the full award. On a national scale, moreover, it remains insignificant. As Figure 5.2 shows, its contribution to the proportion of 17 year olds obtaining an advanced mathematics qualification is tiny.

Figure 5.2 *Maths AS entries in relation to maths A level, 1992–1998*

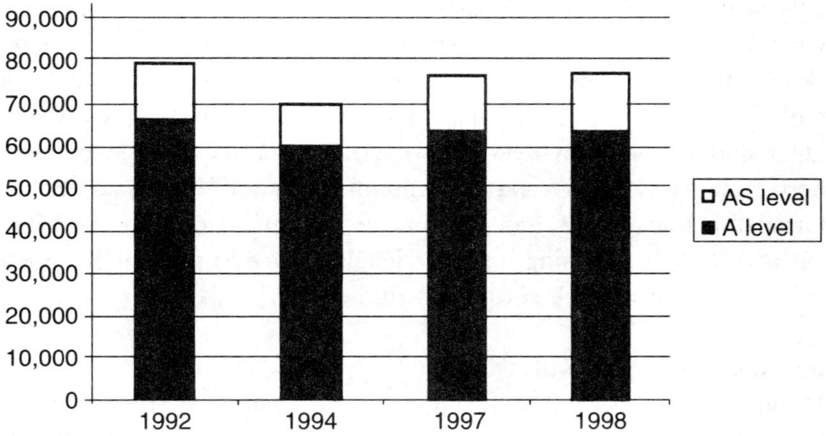

Note: As some candidates take both an AS and an A level in mathematics during their sixth form studies, these figures include an unknown amount of double counting.
Source: DES/DfEE School Examinations Statistics (annual).

Mathematics within A and AS levels
The overwhelming majority of A level pupils have already obtained a C grade or above at GCSE mathematics, and therefore are not resitting their GCSEs. A level and AS level entries consequently show virtually the full extent of post-GCSE mathematics take-up by academic track pupils.

(The same is true in Scotland for Highers students.) Some students will obtain a certain amount of formal mathematics instruction in the context of other subjects (e.g. chemistry or psychology), but this will generally be on an intermittent basis in order to deal with problems arising in the syllabus material. Moreover, the trend in most A level syllabuses has been to reduce any mathematical content in order to make them as accessible as possible to students whose mathematics may extend only as far as the Intermediate tier GCSE content.

Moving from figures on A level passes or entries to conclusions about the actual number of students studying mathematics at A or AS level requires a number of assumptions about numbers entering for both A and AS, or for two mathematics – as opposed to a mathematics and a further mathematics – A levels. Comparisons over time are further complicated by the fact that, in the 1960s, when many students took two mathematics A levels, but others only one, a wide range of options and syllabuses was on offer. Therefore, it is virtually impossible to be sure how many individual students were involved. However, even on the most generous of interpretations, one arrives at a maximum figure for 1997 of 25 per cent of academic track pupils, and just nine per cent of the age cohort (in England and Wales) obtaining a higher level (A or AS) post-GCSE maths qualification during their sixth-form studies.

The situation in Scotland
The wider range of subjects taken by Scottish pupils at Highers (in the equivalent of the lower-sixth year) leads to many more students (proportionately) taking mathematics. However, even there, the majority of the age cohort do not continue with maths through to Higher level. In 1998, for example, almost 60,000 fourth-year students took Standard Grade mathematics (roughly equivalent to GCSE). A year later, in 1999, there were 13,856 Higher Grade mathematics entries, i.e. about 23 per cent of the cohort. However, although the original target year for sitting Highers was the fifth year (S5), more and more students now complete a sixth year, some (the most academic) taking just the Certificate of Sixth Year Studies at its close, but many others taking or retaking Highers. These

later entries brought Higher entry numbers in 1999 up to about 20,000. That is 12 per cent of all Higher grade entries and roughly one-third of the 1998 Standard Grade entry. However, this does not adjust for re-sits: the proportion of the cohort taking Higher maths will thus be rather less than one-third.

Access to mathematics A level

Given that the pool of well-equipped A level candidates in England and Wales only amounts to 17 per cent of GCSE candidates (or 15 per cent of the cohort) the uptake of A/AS level mathematics (at nine per cent of the cohort), is actually quite impressive. It means, in effect, that more than half of those who are equipped to choose the A level do so; not a record most GCSE/A level combinations can equal. Of course, in theory, students who took the Intermediate paper can also proceed to A level. However, they will not have covered a good deal of ground which is implicitly, if not always explicitly, assumed by the A level core, so this is neither an easy nor, usually, a happy choice, and is not one which most institutions encourage. Thus, for most of these students, A level mathematics is effectively precluded from the age of 14 onwards.

Perceptions of mathematics A level

This relative popularity of mathematics A level is the more surprising given that the current A level structure provides powerful incentives to drop mathematics altogether. Sixth-form students, conscious that entry to the most desired universities and courses is highly competitive, feel under pressure to select subjects in which they have done well, and are confident of their future performance. There is, at the same time, a general perception that mathematics A levels are difficult. Carol Fitz-Gibbon's work for the Schools Curriculum Assessment Authority (SCAA) has added strength to this view, arguing that a comparison of the A level grades of students with equivalent GCSE results indicates that mathematics is approximately a grade 'harder' than English (Fitz-Gibbon and Vincent, 1994).

The apparent difficulty of mathematics A level may not matter to students who are sure that mathematics is what they want to study at degree level, as at university entrance they will be competing only against other people who have done the same A level. However, 16 year olds with this degree of certainty are few and far between. On the contrary, research underlines the desire of most young people to keep their options open, and to maximize the number of future routes through higher education and the labour market which they can follow (Wolf, 1997; Boudon, 1982). Moreover, while few schools would actively dissuade a pupil from doing an A level which they were determined on, and could pass, all are acutely aware of the way A levels rankings are calculated, and the effect on their recruitment and image. Active dissuasion may be quite rare; but that is quite different from actively persuading a student to take A levels where high grades seem less assured (and which the school may also perceive as generally more difficult). These pressures make it particularly unlikely that Intermediate-tier maths students will be encouraged to take a mathematics A level.

Incentives for all but the best students to take A level are further reduced by ongoing developments in higher education. As is discussed in Chapter Four, few university courses now feel able to require mathematics A level – and this includes most science, business and even many engineering degrees. For students whose greatest interest is in other areas (e.g. arts and social studies) there is even less incentive, or, often, opportunity to select mathematics. To repeat: it is somewhat surprising, in the circumstances, that as many students take mathematics A level as do. Nonetheless, they amount to a stagnant and small proportion of the age cohort.

The decline of further mathematics A level

The numbers taking further mathematics, i.e. a second mathematics A level, are not stagnant. Instead they are falling steadily from low to tiny numbers, and large swathes of the country's secondary school population do not even have the option of selecting the subject. Cost pressures and the declining numbers of teachers equipped to teach A level mathematics are the main culprits here, rather than league tables – something which makes further decline more or less inevitable under current recruitment and training policies. Table 5.2 summarizes the decline in double mathematics A level entries and the growing inequality of access. Fewer than one in ten mathematics A level entrants now combines this with a further mathematics qualification, and those who do are concentrated in the most privileged institutions, and increasingly so. For the last five years, on average, the independent schools have provided one-seventh of all A level candidates, one-fifth of mathematics A level entries, but one-third of those in further mathematics. Among state schools, the former grant-maintained sector claims a disproportionate share of entries. The further education colleges, by contrast, enter a steadily decreasing percentage of mathematics A level entries – down to six per cent – and only two per cent of further mathematics candidates. Yet these are the main providers of second chance and adult education, and in many city areas effectively the only local sixth-form destination.

Table 5.2 *The decline of further mathematics*

(a) Further maths entries in relation to single-subject maths A level

	(1) 'Further maths' entries (syllabuses with this title)	(2) Separate 'pure' and 'applied' entries (syllabuses with these titles)	(3) Column 1 as % entries for single-subject (combined) syllabuses	(4) Column 1 + 0.5 column 2 as % single-subject entries*
1961	1,390	21,404	7.0	60.1
1970	4,362	25,501	12.6	49.5
1980	6,860	18,706	12.4	29.3
1990	not published in disaggregated form			
1993	5,564	**	8.4	(8.4)
1998	5,563	**	7.9	(7.9)

Notes: *Column 3 definitely underestimates the numbers reaching further mathematics standards, as until quite recently, a common pattern was to teach and examine 'pure' and 'applied' maths, rather than maths and further maths. Column 4 equally certainly overestimates the numbers, by assuming that all candidates for pure or applied also sat the other – which was certainly not the case. However, we have no way of finding out precisely how many did so.

**From 1993 onwards, statistics are kept only in terms of 'maths' and 'further maths'.

(b) Access to further mathematics by selected sectors

Entry Sector	% A level			% Maths A level			% Further Maths		
	Independent	LEA-maintained	Further education	Independent	LEA-maintained	Further education	Independent	LEA-maintained	Further education
1993	17	52	15	20	39	9	33	34	3
1998	n/a	n/a	n/a	22	36	6	33	29	2

Note: Further education excludes sixth-form colleges. LEA-maintained excludes grant-maintained and equivalent categories.

Source: DfEE School Examination Statistics and unpublished QCA statistics.

Non-UK practice: the contrasting picture

Even a cursory survey of international practice makes it evident that the absence of mathematics from the timetables of most English (and many Scottish) 17 year olds is a highly unusual phenomenon. The tendency to build up timetables from individually selected courses and subjects, and to allow some genuine freedom of choice to students, is a characteristic of Anglo-Saxon school systems; but even within this group, no-one else offers either the same degree of free choice or the same degree of sixth-form specialization. Australia, Canada and New Zealand, while continuing to follow many of this country's educational fashions, have parted company with us in this respect. In the United States, high school graduation and college requirements mean that a large part of high school timetables is in effect externally prescribed and common to all students. In continental Europe, the dominant pattern is that of a 'single award' certificate, such as the French baccalauréat or German Abitur. Students must choose one from a limited number of 'bundles' of subjects: and while these allow for some specialization, there is also a high proportion of content common to them all.

The situation in the United States

It is interesting to start with a look at current US practice, as British observers tend to be rather dismissive of US education, at least below university level. This attitude is based partly on the picture of the US high school projected by Hollywood, partly on a visceral dislike of the multiple-choice testing which is the country's most familiar educational artefact, partly on the flood of criticism of their own system which emerges from US commentators, and partly on the fact that US children can generally be relied on to perform (even) worse than British children on international achievement comparisons. (There is a very human tendency to disbelieve and provide critiques of these tests when used to compare our schools with those that apparently do better, but to accept them when the comparison works in our favour.)

However, most Americans stay in general education far longer than their UK counterparts, and they also tend to study maths for much longer. The pick-and-mix credit-based curriculum of high school may allow some students to complete all the required mathematics courses some time before the semester in which they graduate. However, all but a very few students will in fact continue with mathematics until the end or close to the end of high school – not least because of its central importance in the Scholastic Aptitude Tests (SATs) which play a major role in university entrance decisions.

All Americans who graduate from high school, including those who choose a significant number of vocational courses, must meet formal requirements which include mathematics courses. Simply passing the basic courses required to graduate is not hugely demanding, although graduation requirements have been rising steadily during the last decade. The more interesting statistic is for numbers doing a full 'pre-college' curriculum, which have soared. In 1984, only three per cent of high school seniors (i.e. final-year students) were following the full combination of maths, science, social studies and English courses recommended by a government commission; ten years later, the proportion had risen to one-third.

Advanced Placement courses, leading to external examinations of an A level type, and offering college credit, have also grown enormously, and are now taken by three times as many students as in the mid 1980s. While the absolute numbers taking Advanced Placement maths tests remains fairly small, at the equivalent of 64 per thousand twelfth graders (i.e. 6.4 per cent), it is not that much lower than participation in mathematics A level by English sixth formers (National Center for Education Statistics, 1997). While the top students in today's US high schools will certainly have covered much less mathematics than an English student taking mathematics and further mathematics, there are, as we have seen, precious few such students. On the other hand, all college-bound US students will continue to study mathematics for considerably longer than their average English counterpart.

Like English policy-makers, US policy-makers are much occupied with the relatively poor maths performance of their 10 and 14 year olds compared to the countries of the Pacific Rim, and notably Japan, Taiwan, Hong Kong and Singapore. (See especially the results of the recent Third International Mathematics and Science Study (TIMSS): Keys, Harris and Fernandes, 1996, and Brown, 1999.) In none of these Asian countries, however, is this level of achievement seen as adequate and as justification for allowing students to abandon maths at the age of 16, like their UK counterparts. In every single one of the dynamic countries of the Pacific Rim, mathematics constitutes a major compulsory part of the academic curriculum up to university entrance level. In Singapore, over one-quarter of the age cohort are taking A level mathematics, often in conjunction with four other subjects.

The situation in Europe

Finally, for all our claims to be good Europeans, in this area we are strikingly different from any of our EU partners, or, indeed, any other Western or Central European country. In academic upper secondary courses, as noted earlier, almost all European countries operate with a baccalauréat-type system. Subjects are grouped together into packages, which are certificated as a whole. This approach brings with it a curriculum which, in the post-compulsory period, allows for an emphasis on sciences, on mathematics, on foreign languages or on humanities, but which *also requires all students to retain elements of all of these*. In other words, any academic track student will continue to study maths, albeit at differing levels, throughout their secondary school career: and, as a corollary of this, will find their access to university partly dependent on their success in the subject.

Academic track pupils in other European countries, like their UK counterparts, tend to see the maths and science options as difficult (although also, usually, as the most prestigious). Countries differ in how much mathematics specialization they encourage or allow, with only a few countries approaching the level of specialization (or attainment) encompassed by the 'double maths and physics' A level option. Countries also differ in the level of mathematics specified. However, the general trend in Europe and, indeed, worldwide has been to increase the amount and level of mathematics required of students in academic tracks. Certainly, in the countries of which I have first-hand knowledge (which include France, Italy, Germany, the Netherlands and Sweden) any academic track student will progress to levels which go beyond GCSE, and well beyond the requirements for an Intermediate tier C grade.

For example, in France students follow a course which, over several years, leads to a baccalauréat with a particular title/specialism.[6] Everyone in the relevant group follows the same subjects: the choice is between one complete programme and another, with maths compulsory, but differing between programmes. One group of French awards, the baccalauréats professionnels, are designed as labour market entry qualifications rather than as an access route to university, and are discussed further in the next section. By contrast, the huge majority of students selecting an option from among the 'general' or 'technical' baccalauréats are university-bound. In 1997, 53 per cent of the relevant cohort started a general or technical baccalauréat (which they were due to complete in the summer of 2000). All of these students will complete a maths course which covers at least as much ground as an English AS level in mathematics; those selecting a science or maths-oriented general baccalauréat and those in a large proportion of the technical baccalauréat programmes will cover A level maths or more.

Sweden is, by French standards, undemanding in the mathematics syllabuses it prescribes for its academic track upper secondary students; but here too it is unthinkable that any of them should abandon mathematics altogether. The more than 90 per cent of 16 year olds who enter upper secondary education are offered a choice between 16 three-year programmes, three of them academic (with sub-specialisms), 13 of them vocational, and each including the same eight general education subjects as a major part of the programme. What all these programmes share, however, is a core of general education, including mathematics; and mathematics is allocated a minimum of several hours a week.[7] The mathematics syllabus is divided into sequential segments, and the amount that must be covered depends on the programme – thus all students must cover at least programme A mathematics, but after that, there is differentiation. All academic track students, even those specializing in literature and humanities, must cover at least programmes A and B, which, again, takes them well beyond GCSE, as well as ensuring that they do not fall back to levels below those achieved at the age of 16, and the vast majority add C; scientists add D and E as well.

Some of these non-UK students would probably quite like to give up maths, and cannot because their countries have embraced the idea of a broad, balanced curriculum through to the end of secondary education. However, it is not obvious that they are less 'free' in their choices than English, or even Scottish, students. Many of our young people feel similarly constrained, forced to choose only three subjects when they would prefer five, six or more. Moreover, US, European, Asian and Australasian students are making *far fewer permanent, irrevocable decisions about their future careers than are 16 years olds in England*.[8]

To other Europeans, the idea that the vast majority of students should cease to receive any formal mathematics instruction after the equivalent of our year 11 would seem quite extraordinary. The pronounced difference between the UK and the rest of Europe is the more extraordinary because for younger students there has been a marked convergence of practice. In every country there is now a commitment to a broad, common curriculum for all young people up to the end of compulsory schooling; and an emphasis on ensuring flexibility, and providing a variety of pathways to higher level studies. In the 16–19 age group, however, the

UK is more clearly the odd one out than in any previous part of this century. It has pursued a completely different approach and done so in vocational as well as academic teaching, as the next section explains in greater detail.

Mathematics in vocational qualifications

The mathematics discussed so far has been that of the mainstream academic curriculum: the final few years (Key Stage 4) of the National Curriculum years, covering compulsory schooling, and the A level based curriculum, followed in the sixth form or equivalent years by the large majority of young people aspiring to university education. However, a significant number of young people also follow full-time courses of a vocational or semi-vocational nature; others enter apprenticeships straight after taking their GCSEs (or Standard Grade in Scotland); and yet others go onto publicly funded training schemes. Table 5.3 summarizes the main alternatives. As noted above, the main, and very powerful, predictor of which route

Table 5.3 *Main routes post-16: England and Wales*

Age 16-17	% participating	
	1988	**1998**
A/AS	27	36
Other full-time education: e.g. BTEC diplomas, GNVQs (from 1993), GCSE resits	12	24
Full-time vocational education	14	11
Part-time and work-based training, of which:		
Youth training and equivalent	20	6
Modern apprenticeship	n/a	3
Other part-time (including employer-funded training)	8	7
Other: in work but not training *or* not in education, training or the labour force	19	13

Source: Department for Education and Employment (1999), *Participation in Education and Training by 16–18 year olds in England and Wales 1988–1998.*

a young person enters at age 16 is their GCSE results. Maths GCSE (or more specifically, whether the critical C grade is attained) operates as an especially important influence on whether someone will enter the A level route.

Mathematics in general vocational courses

A very high proportion of those following full-time vocational courses (Advanced GNVQs, Business and Technician Education Council (BTEC) Nationals) aspire to university. For example, in a large-scale study of GNVQ students (Further Education Development Agency, 1997) well over half the respondents saw their courses as a route to higher education or advanced specialist training (e.g. nursing). Others, notably a high proportion of those in apprenticeships or on craft vocational courses in further education (e.g. construction, catering, motor mechanics and craft engineering), are likely to enter occupations where broad mathematical competence is highly important.

Given the weak skills with which students enter, one might expect that mathematics would figure large in the design of these courses. In a sense it does. Unfortunately, the approach adopted – by the UK, but especially by the English – is unique in a number of ways and has become increasingly rather than decreasingly distinctive over the last 15 years. In the economy as a whole, completely new products are the exception and the vast majority of them fail totally. The current approach to mathematics in vocational courses is, in my view, one of those product failures, but one which its architects and overseers are hugely reluctant to acknowledge.

Over the last few decades there has been, in the UK, a powerful movement of opposition to separate maths teaching in vocational courses. This opposition is closely bound up with a 'progressive' philosophy of education (Bates, 1998) which emphasizes the presumed superiority, both motivationally and in terms of effective learning, of embedding the teaching of mathematics in the teaching of practical applications rather than treating it separately. The assumption is that any separate maths teaching will be 'dry' and overtly theoretical. In policy-making groups (such as the government quangos who oversee vocational awards) the most favoured argument for integration is that separate teaching will mean that colleges end up teaching maths on a wet Friday afternoon to a group of discontented trainee butchers ... a situation whose horror is self-evident enough to condemn the whole approach.

Instead, the full integration of mathematics into vocational content is encouraged. Assessment of the old craft courses organized by City and Guilds, which dominated craft training until the 1980s, generally included separate maths papers, dealing with applied calculations and operations. However, the courses run by BTEC, which became a major part of post-compulsory education in the 1970s and 1980s, pioneered the alternative integrated approach (while retaining separate maths units for most science, engineering and technology subjects).

All of these BTEC courses – including those with separate maths units – were required to incorporate 'common skills' which included numeracy. At the same time, these common skills had no specific standards or assessment requirements attached to them. Not surprisingly, therefore, many of the course teams responsible for developing and delivering a given course tended to pay them little attention except when writing reports to BTEC to 'demonstrate' that the common skills had been covered as part of other (syllabus-led) modules. Other 'general' or 'pre-vocational' courses (e.g. the Certificate of Pre Vocational Education (CPVE) and the Diploma in Vocational Education (DVE))[9] took a similar approach with similar results (Wolf, 1992). Mathematics was integrated into oblivion.

Mathematics within vocational training programmes

In the mid 1980s the government undertook a massive reform of vocational education which resulted in an equally massive boost for the integrated approach to mathematics teaching. The National Council for Vocational Qualifications (NCVQ) was set up in order to introduce a national framework for what was seen as a 'jungle' of vocational qualifications. The Council created a detailed 'methodology' (sic.) for any award recognized as a National Vocational Qualification (NVQ), and its directives had an immediate and widespread impact on the more applied and practical vocational awards – including all the traditional City and Guilds craft courses, which, under government pressure, were rapidly converted into NVQs.

NVQs have tended to comprise long lists of very narrowly defined practical competencies, all of which must be assessed and recorded, for the most part in applied workplace situations. Correspondingly, the NCVQ set itself firmly against the creation of separately assessed modules (units or elements) dealing with general skills and knowledge, such as mathematics. Any assessment of mathematics other than in the context of use was inauthentic, and could not count towards the final assessment and acquisition of these 'competence-based' awards. Instead, the lecturer or trainer has been expected to infer mathematical requirements from the 'performance criteria' which specify the final outcome of occupational competence, and encouraged to deliver any such mathematics as an integral part of the vocational training proper.

NVQs' creators believed this would promote more effective mathematics teaching, as the lecturers and trainers would ensure that any mathematics implied by the 'performance criteria' would be taught and tested through applications. NVQs therefore went even further down the road of 'integration' than had the BTEC diplomas without any independent specification of mathematical requirements at all. Many of the older City and Guilds craft courses, which had separate mathematics papers, disappeared at this time. So, on the whole, did most mathematics teaching for these students.

Steedman and Hawkins, for example, report that, in construction, the move to NVQs has 'resulted in a training programme ... which requires the demonstration of competence in only the most basic mathematical operations'. Around two-thirds of the topics required for the old-style, formally examined City and Guilds courses had disappeared from the assessors' handbooks used by NVQ assessors in recording and accrediting trainees' performance (Steedman and Hawkins, 1994: 96, 97). A prime-time Channel 4 programme and report, *All Our Futures*, in 1993 strongly attacked the NVQ approach, and gave prominence to experienced individuals from industry, union and training backgrounds who were deeply unhappy with the way in which separate teaching and testing of mathematics and technology were being phased out of craft awards such as those for plumbers and electricians. For example, a college head of department complained that NVQs were 'only calling for a superficial explanation to be given' rather than testing substantive knowledge of technical mathematics (Channel 4, 1993).

The NVQ approach does not actually forbid trainers to set time aside to teach mathematics and other subjects separately; but it gives them little or no incentive to do so. In a crowded timetable where huge numbers of practical competences have to be assessed and recorded one by one, and where written examinations are stigmatized, any formal teaching of mathematics – and that includes the teaching of craft applications – is rapidly squeezed out. In the case of competences which appear to require mathematics (e.g. 'Discrepancies in claims for payment are investigated and resolved' or 'Stock requirements are accurately calculated') it is not beyond the power of most assessors to find instances where that mathematics is not too demanding. Steedman and Hawkins note that a careful analysis of carpentry NVQs, as delivered in further education colleges, showed that 'the implicit mathematics is ... far more demanding than the mathematics the candidate is (actually) required to show understanding of to gain NVQ certification' (Steedman and Hawkins, 1994: 96).

The consequences of this approach for young people's progression were never a live issue, because the essence of NVQs was that they certificated particular levels of workplace competence. They were never designed or intended to be part of a graduated training route or means of accessing further education. Nonetheless, they were made, and remain, the qualification offered to young people on government-funded training schemes – a group which is generally drawn from among the least qualified 16 year olds.

The government originally envisaged all vocational courses becoming NVQs, but the major and growing demand from 16–18 year olds was for courses with a more general orientation, offering pathways into higher education. Far from flocking to NVQs, they have continued, in increasing numbers, to remain in full-time education. As we saw earlier, ever-larger numbers have progressed into A level courses. Parallel to this, there has been a growth in the numbers entering full-time classroom-based courses which can be most accurately characterized as semi-vocational or as vocational preparation. BTEC awards exemplify this type of courses. In the early 1990s, faced with the fact that such courses were not, as predicted, being abandoned for NVQs, the government introduced GNVQs. Their approach was closer to the BTEC model than was the case with NVQs; but, unlike BTEC awards, they are designed to be delivered in schools as readily as in further education colleges.

Key skills

At the time of their introduction and design – a task which the government handed over to the NCVQ – the possibility of developing separate units in maths, English and foreign languages was considered. In the end, however, GNVQs embraced the ideal of integration for English, information technology (IT) skills and all mathematics teaching. This was done through a development of the BTEC common skills idea. Every GNVQ course required the assessment and certification of 'core skills'. These covered a number of areas, including *application of number*, and all were supposed to be taught and assessed in an integrated fashion, as part of the content of the vocational units. To date, the only GNVQ with a compulsory separate mathematics unit is engineering (at the insistence of the Engineering Employers Federation).

Following the Dearing Report on post-16 education (Dearing, 1996), the core skills were re-named 'key skills', but otherwise remained essentially unchanged. Whether core or key, the skills are exactly the same for all vocational areas. There is no attempt to alter the list to fit a different vocational context; rather the contextualization is meant to come from their integration, by teachers, into ongoing subject-specific work. They also come at a number of different levels. The level at which these skills are delivered is not tied to the award; in theory, students studying for a Level 3 GNVQ could be working to obtain/being accredited with Level 4 key skills. In practice, this does not happen. Key skills are certified at whatever the level is of the GNVQ as a whole (Further Education Development Agency, 1997).

Due to the nature of the assessment regime (which requires evidence of coverage for every single part of the specifications) and due to fact that the list of skills for number includes quite a long list of highly specific mathematics operations, the application of number requirements have tended to be taken rather more seriously than their predecessors, the BTEC common skills. In fact, the impossibility of covering many of them in an integrated way, within the vocational curriculum, has led most schools and colleges to set aside some separate time for application of number. How this is done, what is covered in separate and what in the (recommended) integrated teaching, what materials are used for teaching, how much time is allocated – all these are entirely the decision of the individual centre.

Evaluation and development of key skills
A number of evaluations and reports on key skills have now appeared (e.g. Further Education Development Agency, 1995, 1997; Office for Standards in Education, 1994, 2000; Further Education Funding Council, 1994). While they do not, in general, remark on the singularity of the approach, and the extent to which it is out of line with international practice, they are consistent in reporting major problems with delivery, especially in application of number and IT. There is enormous variation in delivery patterns; many of the vocational teachers, who are charged with teaching, assessing and accrediting key skill achievement, express concern over their abilities in an area for which they have never been trained or prepared. Inspectors observe that coverage is often weak, and students not taken beyond the level they had attained in previous GCSE work (Office for Standards in Education, 1994). It should also be emphasized that the level of the 'key skills' requirements in mathematics is not high. A new modular mathematics GCSE for adults being offered by Mathematics in Education and Industry also provides an accreditation facility for key skills. Even the 'Advanced' level (Level 3) application of number requirements are provided for through just half of the Intermediate tier GCSE syllabus.

The problems with key skills delivery almost certainly underlie a major recent change in government policy. From autumn 2000 onwards, key skills are being 'uncoupled'. In other words, although students will be strongly encouraged to take the key skills, they will no longer have to achieve them in order to obtain their certificate. The official explanation is that GNVQ students were disadvantaged, as they bore an additional burden which A level students do not, and could fail a GNVQ in which their subject expertise was great just because of a key skills failure. While true in theory, such an event is actually so rare that none of the main awarding bodies can actually cite an example. The policy change thus appears to be largely a response to the lack of credibility currently attached to key skills as a certification of anything.

However, the English government has not, in the process, abandoned its commitment to the key skills approach. On the contrary, many millions of pounds are being poured into developing and marketing a curious and completely unique 'key skills qualification', involving three subjects – communication, IT and application of number. The basic philosophy of total integration remains: these key skills (see Figure 5.3) are to be demonstrated through the medium of other work produced in the course of other studies, and largely assessed by the students' teachers. However there is also to be some external assessment, which in the case of application of number consists of a standard numeracy test, reminiscent of a rather easy GCSE paper, and covering the arithmetical and some of the data analysis elements in Foundation and Intermediate tier GCSE. Thus, we have a qualification combining a philosophy of total integration with some decontextualized numeracy. While institutions will no longer be obliged to offer 'key skills' to their vocational students, they will be strongly encouraged to do so (e.g. through the funding mechanism whereby funds follow qualifications).[10]

Overall, therefore, mathematics teaching in English vocational courses is quite as unique as it is for academic courses; indeed, perhaps more so, as in the former it is simply missing, while in the latter we find features and delivery patterns totally different from those used anywhere else in the world. Particularly striking is the combination of a completely 'common'

Figure 5.3 *Key skills – application of number level 3 (part of the new AS equivalent qualification), extracts from the specification*

What is this unit about?
This unit is about applying your number skills in a substantial and complex activity.

You will show you can:

- plan, and interpret information from different sources;
- carry out multi-stage calculations;
- present findings, explain results and justify your choice of methods.

In planning an activity and interpreting information, you need to know how to:

- plan a substantial and complex activity by breaking it down into a series of tasks;
- obtain relevant information from different sources, including a large data set (over 50 items), and use this to meet the purpose of your activity;
- (and six other requirements)

In carrying out calculations, you need to know how to:

- show your methods clearly and work to appropriate levels of accuracy;
- carry out multi-stage calculations with numbers of any size (e.g. find the results of growth at 8% over three years, find the volume of water in a swimming pool);
- use powers and roots (e.g. work out interest on £5,000 at 5% over three years);
- (and six other requirements)

Evidence must show you can:

- plan how to obtain and use the information required to meet the purpose of your activity;
- obtain the relevant information; and
- choose appropriate methods for obtaining the results you need and justify your choice,
- carry out calculations to appropriate levels of accuracy, clearly showing your methods;
- check methods and results to help ensure errors are found and corrected,
- select appropriate methods of presentation and justify your choice;
- present your findings effectively; and
- explain how the results of your calculations relate to the purpose of your activity.

GUIDANCE
Examples of activities you might use
You will have opportunities to develop and apply your number skills during your work, studies or other activities. For example, when:

- planning, carrying out and reporting findings from a substantial investigation or project;
- designing, making and presenting a product;
- researching information and explaining the outcomes to customers or clients.

You will need time to practise your skills and prepare for assessment. So it is important to plan ahead.

Source: Qualitifations and Curriculum Authority: Key Skills Specifications.

list of skills, the same across all vocational areas, with an emphasis on completely integrated delivery. Also unusual are the absence of any guidance on time to be spent on teaching and learning mathematics, the uncoupling (in theory) of key skill and award levels, and the degree to which the design of teaching and assessment materials are delegated to the individual teacher or course team.

Non-UK practice – the contrasting picture

At first sight, the vocational curriculum in the UK may look closer to the international pattern. In some cases, this is indeed the case. Many older, traditional vocational awards and one of the newer ones (the engineering GNVQ) contain compulsory mathematics units with a vocational emphasis; in other words, they follow the pattern common in, for example, France, Germany or the Netherlands. However, as discussed above, in most cases the UK's vocational curriculum offers mathematics only under a different name and with a very distinctive – indeed, unique – 'integrated' approach.

Mathematics in non-UK general vocational courses

By contrast, the general international approach to mathematics in vocational and technical education is to teach the subject separately, but using specialized curricula which differ between courses and are suited to a particular occupation or group of occupations. Countries give greater or lesser emphasis to using the mathematics in an applied way. Thus, while some teach mathematics to vocational students in a rather abstract fashion, in other countries the maths, although delivered separately, is taught in an overwhelmingly 'contextualized' way.

However, while pedagogical philosophy and style may vary, vocational courses outside the UK *consistently include mathematics as a compulsory element and equally consistently allocate it a separate place in the timetable.*[11] Moreover, in all European Union countries other than the UK, there has been a marked trend, over the last 15 years, to increase the general education component in these vocational programmes. This involves giving more time to the traditional central subjects of the school curriculum: mathematics, own-language expertise and a foreign language. The 'modal' European vocational track student is receiving significantly more general education than was the case 10 or 15 years ago, which includes an upgrading of the mathematical content and requirements of the programme (Green, Wolf and Leney, 1999). This means more time devoted explicitly to mathematics.

Rising aspirations and rising staying-on rates at both upper secondary and college/university levels mean that many 'vocational' courses are now best seen as semi-vocational, or an alternative form of general education for the less academically successful. In these programmes, the possibility of progression is critically important to students, and this in itself tends to lead (outside the UK) to more emphasis on mathematics, own language studies, science and foreign languages. The two countries described in most detail earlier – France and Sweden – exemplify this trend. In the French vocational baccalauréats, there is an emphasis both on mathematical applications and on advanced mathematics: both are taught and both are examined. In Sweden the tradition is one of teacher assessment, and the maths required of vocational programme students is less theoretical than in France. Nonetheless, the design of these programmes includes explicit provision for students to progress to university and a large general education component, including completion of specified levels of the upper secondary mathematics curriculum referred to above. As Swedish upper secondary maths provision is conceptualized in a unitary way, covering all students, the different levels lead into each other. All vocational students must complete the A course (with a minimum of 100 teaching hours). Many then proceed onto B. Those wishing to enter technical higher education may go on to C (and so on).

Mathematics in non-UK vocational training

An emphasis on explicit mathematics teaching is also found in other countries' apprenticeship and training systems. A series of detailed case-studies by the National Institute of Economic and Social Research (NIESR) (see especially Steedman and Hawkins, 1994; Prais, 1991; Wolf, 1992) have documented the very different experiences of young people in UK vocational training as compared to other major European countries. Young British construction trainees, for example, cover a far more restricted range of mathematics skills than German apprentices, whose mathematics lessons are highly contextualized, but also separately specified and delivered. A member of the UK's Institute of Plumbing, visiting the Netherlands in 1993, noted: 'In Holland plumbing apprentices are dealing with fairly demanding trigonometry within their first week of the course. We never ever get on to trigonometry. In the 1950s and 1960s we did, but not now.' (Channel 4, 1993)

One reason why our European Union partners insist on including substantial amounts of maths within apprenticeship is that it offers apprentices the possibility of progressing to higher training in polytechnics and universities – a possibility which they recognize as not only beneficial to existing apprentices, but as crucial if apprenticeships are to remain attractive. Current upper secondary reforms in the United States are designed to improve the traditional vocational track in high schools. They too, ensure that all reformed vocational options also provide for progression to college (Organisation for Economic Cooperation and Development, 1999). Britain's Skills Task Force is strongly supportive of apprenticeship (Skills Task Force, 1999). It recognizes the need for our system to offer progressive routes if it is to survive, let alone grow. However, the current Modern Apprenticeship regime of NVQs plus key skills signally fails to promote such patterns – especially not in technical areas where mathematics is a necessity, not an option.

Is our current approach working?

What matters is not whether a country does things in the same way as the rest of the world, but whether its approach is working. The evidence indicates very strongly that the English approach is not.

Let us start with the vocational students described in the previous section. The absence of separate mathematics requirements (and active discouragement of separate mathematics lessons) is derived from the belief that maths should be related to the contexts in which it is used. It is absolutely true that students who are taught abstract maths in isolation often have enormous difficulty in applying and using mathematics. That means the application is more difficult. It does *not* mean that they are going to find things easier if they are never taught the maths at all. Moreover, *there is no reason why encouraging mathematics applications and vocationally relevant techniques need preclude separate mathematics teaching.* Indeed, one of the most puzzling aspects of the current key skills approach is the fact that the skills are not in any way 'vocationally specific'. It is also extraordinary that the introduction of this completely novel idea has occurred without any sort of targeted or large-scale training programme for the teachers involved.

Summary of post-compulsory mathematics in England

Studies of English vocational students' skills invariably show that, as a group, they have serious mathematics problems. (See, for example, Rudd and Steedman, 1997; Wolf and Rapiau, 1993.) As most academic-stream English students drop mathematics, we have little evidence regarding this group's levels of achievement. What we do know are the following facts.

1. A very large proportion of students who take the middle-level GCSE papers finish their compulsory schooling with little or no knowledge of, say, algebra or geometry.
2. A level students in this situation have their choice of degree course circumscribed; so too do vocational track students using their awards as a route to higher education.
3. Many students with limited mathematics preparation nonetheless continue onto courses which are relatively 'mathematics heavy'. Chapter Four describes in detail the consequences of this for the quality of our degree programmes, and for the students' learning.
4. Many pupils taking GNVQs will only have completed bottom-tier GCSE papers. This may include a considerable number of Advanced GNVQ candidates, as half of the latter do an Intermediate GNVQ first, before starting their Advanced course. The mathematical skills of this group are very poor – significantly poorer than, say, their Swedish

counterparts at this age (Wolf and Steedman, 1998). Yet while some will re-take GCSE, many others will receive only what is offered through 'key skills' – guaranteeing that the gap which exists at 16 will be wider still at 18 or 19 years of age.

5. A level students are, from the year 2000, being encouraged to take a larger number of subjects than at present, by taking a set of AS levels in the first year of the sixth form and then taking a subset of these on to A level the following year. This reform may or may not be more successful than the previous AS level development; indications are that most schools will encourage students to take four rather than three subjects, but no more. In any case, an AS in maths will remain a risky and therefore unattractive choice for students who have not completed the upper tier at GCSE (i.e. the vast majority of students).

6. The only officially endorsed and promoted strategy for improving the mathematics of the rest of the age group is the key skills qualification in which number applications make up one-third of the content. Although the Qualifications and Curriculum Authority (QCA) has approved some stand-alone maths qualifications for the post-16 market, these have not been a part of any government/Department for Education and Employment (DfEE) strategy and their future is unclear.

International comparisons

The contrast with recent European and, indeed, worldwide trends is astonishing. As described above, other countries have been increasing the mathematics requirements of both academic and vocational programmes in recent years, and ensuring that all students continue to receive instruction in new areas. Of course, it remains a possibility that the rest of the world has got it wrong and the British have got it right: not so much in the approach to teaching mathematics, but on the question of whether post-compulsory students actually need any mathematics at all. Once again, however, one must conclude that the evidence is otherwise.

There is now a growing body of convincing, international evidence to the effect that unskilled workers in developed countries face a very uncertain future (see, for example, Wood, 1994; Ashton and Green,

1996). Throughout the industrialized world, the more highly educated receive higher incomes, and enjoy more secure employment; conversely, those with few or no qualifications are increasingly marginalized. It is difficult to separate out the extent to which this is because education has actually increased productivity, rather than because employers use education as a filtering device; but there is a substantial body of evidence, discussed in Chapter Two, which suggests that low levels of literacy and numeracy, in particular, have long-term effects on people's success in work and their life chances.

The mathematics we need
Of course, this does not prove that higher levels of *mathematical* skill and understanding are required; and, indeed, there were people who argued that the advent of the calculator would liberate schools to reduce the size and content of the mathematics syllabus enormously. Such arguments are rarely heard today, but in the UK discussion is dominated instead by the issue of 'numeracy', narrowly defined. This is apparent in school policy, even more so post-16, where the minimal requirements of a 'key skill' called application of *number* is apparently all we wish to offer most young people. Yet 'numeracy', in this number skills sense, forms only a small part of the mathematics syllabuses followed by most post-compulsory students around the world, and only a small part of mathematics in use too.

As is demonstrated in Chapter Seven, the mathematical demands of the workplace have not been diminished by the advent of calculators, computers, mathematical software, etc. Instead, the latter have enabled people to introduce new, more efficient techniques and working patterns which make use of these machines, and call for new levels of mathematical and statistical understanding. One of the defining characteristics of the extraordinarily productive world economy of the early twenty-first century is the way in which technical progress works by constant improvement of what exists already. It is hardly plausible to suppose that this has stopped, that we can say with confidence that the level of mathematics attained by English 16 year olds is enough for this next century, and other countries are wrong to emphasize the need to upgrade their mathematics curricula.

On the contrary, evidence from this country and from others demonstrates the way in which substantive skills, and not merely paper qualifications, command labour market returns – and are doing so at an increasing rate. Chapter Three details how important A level mathematics has become. Many employers are quite unaware of who, in their workforce, holds an A level in mathematics, but the value of the skills it develops shows up clearly in the wages they pay. In the United States, a series of studies (summarized in Pryor and Schaffer, 1999) confirm the growing importance of skills and the especial importance of mathematical expertise.

Our politicians and policy-makers proclaim the importance of the knowledge society and of 'skilling' our population. Looking at our mathematics education, one wonders if they are serious. What seems only too likely is that the most privileged, ever attuned to the demands of the market, will ensure that their own children are well equipped. The independent schools, whose share in mathematics A and AS levels is already far greater than their A level share overall, will increase take up yet further. The less privileged will be left with qualifications whose rhetoric disguises emptiness. This is bad for them and bad for the country – to be so out of step with the whole developed world is, for once, unambiguously a cause for shame.

Notes

Research for this chapter was partially carried out in conjunction with the Nuffield Foundation-funded project 'Mathematics for All'. The Foundation's support is gratefully acknowledged.

1. Not all syllabuses follow this pattern, but the vast and growing majority of candidates are covered by these arrangements. The current consultation on the National Curriculum proposes two quite distinct programmes of study for the years covered by GCSE preparation. This may also affect the future organization of the GCSE exams.

2. This figure excludes data for students taking the London (ULEAC) examinations as they do not report results by tier, but includes all other English and Welsh examining groups.

3. If we adjust current GCSE figures to provide higher level passes as a proportion of the age cohort, we find that 15 per cent of the age cohort is achieving a high-tier pass, compared to the 24 per cent who passed O level in the mid 1980s.

4. All GCSE figures refer to 1998 entries. For GCSE entries as a whole, 55 per cent of passes are at C or above, but the size and nature of entries varies widely between subjects, as do the grade distributions.

5. Note that the figures used for Figure 5.1 do not include Northern Ireland, while those used for Figures 3.1 and 3.2 do.

6. For up-to-date summary statistics on French education, see *L'état de l'école*, published annually by the French Ministry of Education.

7. Subjects in the three-year Swedish upper secondary programme are allocated 'points', which are roughly equivalent to one hour's teaching time apiece. The 'modal' academic track option of A+B+C is currently 200 points, and due to rise to 250 for maths in recognition of the subject's importance.

8. The current Scottish 'Highers', taken at the end of year 12, are in the 'pick and mix' tradition, rather than involving a baccalauréat type programme; but because more subjects are taken, proportionately more students take maths than in England and Wales. The 'Higher Still' reforms will continue this approach and should also lead to more dedicated maths teaching and certification among students who would currently take vocational programmes.

9. These were awarded on the basis of one-year full-time courses taken by rather low-achieving students post-GCSE. Neither ever achieved any discernible market value (Robinson, 1997).

10. The current arrangement is that colleges will get funding equivalent to an AS level if they sign students up to a key skills qualification. This money can and no doubt will be used to top up funding for the students' A levels or GNVQs, through which the key skills are to be 'delivered'. (It is an interesting question how many of these students will actually complete the key skills award: non-entry or failure carries some financial penalty but not a huge one.)

11. I personally do not know of any countries outside the UK where separate mathematics, separately taught, is not part of the school-based vocational courses

6 Constructing Purposeful Mathematical Activity in Primary Classrooms

Janet Ainley
Mathematics Education Research Centre, Institute of Education, University of Warwick

Introduction

In social, political and even educational arenas, mathematics is commonly portrayed as a subject whose importance is based on its usefulness in employment and daily life.

> Mathematics is only 'useful' to the extent to which it can be applied to a particular situation. (Cockcroft, 1982: para. 249)

This justification of mathematics continues to be acknowledged at least in a token way in the construction of the mathematics curriculum in the UK, despite a considerable body of research, as reflected in this book, which indicates the gaps which may exist between the content and practices of school mathematics, and the uses of mathematics in the adult world.

Justifying primary school mathematics

In constructing a mathematics curriculum for primary schools, justifying the learning of mathematics in terms of its usefulness is particularly problematic. The applications of mathematics in the adult world as they are sometimes portrayed in school textbooks (e.g. shopping, gardening, DIY and cooking) are generally far removed from the concerns of young children. Furthermore, the 'realism' of such contexts may be considerably undermined by the need to simplify the quantities and operations involved in order to bring them within the scope of the primary curriculum. Thus, there is a gap between the experiences of children learning mathematics and the purposes that are portrayed for that learning by curriculum materials and by society.

A second kind of 'usefulness' for the mathematics taught in primary schools is that it is a foundation for the mathematics to be taught later, in secondary school. As a justification for learning mathematics, this is equally inaccessible to young children, beyond having a general sense that 'You need to know this when you are in the juniors/Ms Y's class/the secondary school.'

A coherent understanding

Attempts to justify the learning/teaching of mathematics only in terms of its usefulness in the real world, or as a foundation for future learning, seem to me to be inadequate. For one thing, they ignore cultural, aesthetic and logical aspects of mathematics which are essential elements of children's educational entitlement, and reduce mathematics to an arid field of 'numeracy'. Of course, mathematics is an important life skill, but what is important in life is not simply to be able to do particular bits of mathematics, but to have a understanding of how those bits of mathematics are related, and of when and how they might be useful.

In contrast to the precise, hierarchical image which is often assigned to mathematics, this kind of understanding of mathematics tends to be broad and fuzzy, requiring a holistic perspective. Purely utilitarian justifications for the teaching of mathematics tend to lead to a curriculum which fails to offer opportunities for young children to make any sense of the purposes of mathematical knowledge and activity. The ways in which children construct the purpose of mathematical activity in the classroom may have significant effects on their learning of mathematics, and thus may have important implications for both teaching and curriculum development.

In this chapter I want to explore an issue which I feel has received little attention: the question of what sense children make of the experience of learning mathematics, and why they think they are learning it. I begin with a critique of traditional approaches to trying to provide a purpose for mathematics through links with the real world, and explore the ways in which primary children's perceptions of school mathematics may differ from those of their teachers. In the second part of the chapter, I shall examine alternative ways in which the term 'real' might be interpreted, and point to the dangers associated with too narrow an interpretation. Finally, I shall offer a different perspective on mathematical activity which highlights the importance of *purpose* in mathematical learning.

Contextualizing mathematics

In curriculum materials, mathematical activities are often presented in contexts relating to real world situations through the use of word problems. Contextualizing the abstract content of mathematics, presumably to make it more accessible, has a long history. Examples of word problems from primary school textbooks used by our parents or grandparents are often entertaining to modern readers because of their use of pre-decimal currency, and the social setting portrayed. The following example is from *Right from the Start Arithmetic*, first published in 1937.

> Father gave mother £5 to buy overcoats for Jack, Tom and Frank. Mother gave him back £1, 3s. 6d. The coats were all the same price, how much did each cost?   (Schonell and Cracknell, 1937)

A modern example uses a different context, but otherwise is surprisingly similar.

> Four people paid £72 for football tickets. What was the cost of each ticket? How much change did they get from £100?
>   (Department for Education and Employment, 1999)

Apart from the superficial similarities of structure, and the mathematical similarities in the calculations required, these two examples also share an important feature common to the majority of word problems offered in primary school texts. They are set within a familiar context, but there is no purpose offered for the calculations required to answer them. Indeed, as a moment's reflection makes clear, the answer to the central question – the cost of the individual items – must already have been known in order to construct the question. In the real world situation it is not this calculation but its inverse, that is finding the total cost, which is more likely to make sense.

Word problems such as these draw on supposedly real world contexts, but fail to reflect the *purposes* for which mathematics may be used within those same contexts in everyday life. Therefore, it is unclear how much attention should be paid to the context when answering the question. If you actually wanted to know the cost of each coat or each ticket (presumably having forgotten this information since making the purchase), then a sensible strategy in real life would be to look at the till receipt on which the details of the transaction are given. But in the mathematics classroom, that part of the real world context has been omitted.

Applying mathematical knowledge

There has been a considerable amount of research in mathematics education into the difficulties which children have in applying mathematical knowledge, and particularly in combining mathematical and 'real world' knowledge appropriately in answering word problems (see, for example, Boaler, 1993; Verschaffel, De Corte and Borghart, 1996). These difficulties manifest themselves in a number of ways. Children may ignore the context completely, giving answers which are inappropriate. A well known problem used in a number of research studies (National Association of Educational Progress, 1983) involves calculating the number of buses required for taking a certain number of people on an outing. This problem appears in many forms, for example:

> 196 children and 15 adults went on a school trip. Buses seat 57 people.
> How many buses were needed?
>> (Department for Education and Employment, 1999)

Many children will give the answer 3, 3 remainder 40 or 3.70175 – responses which are mathematically 'sensible', but fail to take account of the constraints of the context.

Problems also occur when children use too much real world knowledge in answering word problems. For example, when answering a question which involves finding the price of a can of Coke, some children may give the price they paid the previous day at the corner shop (Cooper, 1998).

Difficulties in applying knowledge

It seems that applying mathematical knowledge appropriately to solve problems is a considerable area of difficulty, not just for children learning mathematics, but in contexts in adult life. Hughes, Desforges and Mitchell (2000) begin their detailed exploration of this issue by making a comparison between difficulties in mathematics and the relative ease with which skills in reading, and in performing other practical tasks, are applied to new contexts.

> There are many other cases where we learn something in a particular setting and transfer our learning readily to other contexts. For example, the first time we see someone using a hammer to knock a nail into wood the circumstances are very particular ... . Most of us, however, are able to generalize our informal lesson in hammering. We are able, without further tuition, to use hammers of all kinds ... . Where a proper hammer is not to hand, we invent substitutes. (Hughes, Desforges and Mitchell, 2000, 5–6)

One essential difference between reading and hammering, and mathematics, which Hughes, Desforges and Mitchell do not discuss, is that when we learn to read or hammer in nails, the *purpose* of those activities is made clear to us. We learn to read in order to be able to read books, magazines, teletext, instructions, signs and advertisements; we hammer in nails to join things together or to hang pictures. When children learn a piece of mathematics, however, is it not always easy for them to understand the purpose of that knowledge, and consequently knowing how and when to apply that knowledge is much more difficult.

How do children make sense of school mathematics?

Children's construction of purpose

In much of my research into the views of children and their teachers about mathematical activities, I have found a number of differences in the perceptions children and teachers have of the nature and purpose of the activity they are engaged in. It seems to me that in many classrooms, and for much of the time, children have different perceptions of the purposes of mathematical activities from those of their teachers. This affects the ways in which they see mathematical tasks, and the ways in which they interpret teachers' behaviour. As a result, teachers and pupils may be working at cross purposes, and teachers may see children's responses as demonstrating a lack of understanding, or of attention, or even as deliberate subversion of the objective of the lesson. However, it also seems clear to me that children work hard at making sense of mathematical activity, even when they are given little basis on which to do this. They construct purposes for their activities within the context of their experience of the classroom and the school, even though they often fail to appreciate the wider purposes which teachers and curriculum developers intend to convey in the ways in which tasks are contextualized. Often these mis-matches arise because children, and sometimes their teachers, are not able to distinguish those aspects of mathematics which are matters of convention from more significant mathematical concepts. I shall offer two examples to illustrate this point.

Example 1: Estimation

The first example is from a lesson I observed a number of years ago which I think is typical of many primary school lessons on measurement (Ainley, 1991). The activity was a familiar one. The children were measuring using foot-lengths as a non-standard unit, and were equipped with 'feet' cut from paper. On the blackboard was a grid:

Object	My estimate	Measurement	Error

The children worked busily on this activity, using a variety of approaches. Some measured each object and then entered the value they obtained in both the 'estimate' and the 'measurement' columns. Some groups agreed on an estimate by discussion, with no apparent reference to the object in question. Some wrote their friend's measurement for an object as their estimate. A few took the task of estimating seriously, but were worried about having 'errors'.

For the teacher, the purpose of this lesson was for children to learn to estimate and measure in non-standard units, which are important real life skills. She also hoped that they would start to see why these units have limited usefulness, and to understand the need for standard units. For the children this was an enjoyable lesson. There was a clearly defined and not-too-difficult task. Their aim was to complete the table they had been given to the teacher's satisfaction, and they used a number of strategies to do this.

However, the teacher's objectives for this lesson were far from being achieved. For the children, the purpose of learning to estimate was never clear; indeed, it is hard to see how it could be, given that the way in which they were using estimation was so different from its uses in everyday life. They were asked to estimate *and then* measure. This makes little sense if you actually want to know the size of something, when estimating and measuring would be alternative strategies. Similarly, the issue of the appropriateness of the units never arose for children because nothing in the activity focused their attention on this. My analysis of the children's behaviour is not that the children were being lazy, or wilfully disobedient; rather they were responding in quite reasonable ways to the constructions they had made of the purpose of the activity.

Example 2: Graphing with spreadsheets

My second example is taken from more recent research into children's use of spreadsheets (Ainley and Pratt, 1995). When children were first introduced to the graphing facilities of a spreadsheet, they were interested in exploring the range of graphs they could produce, and the graphic effects offered by the software. When it came to selecting a graph to print out for inclusion in their project folders, many children made choices which surprised us. They seem to be guided solely by the visual appearance of the graph, and paid no attention to whether or not the graph they had chosen displayed the data appropriately.

Our first interpretation of this behaviour was to feel impatient with children who seemed to be 'playing' with the software, rather than paying attention to the mathematics. When we questioned them about their graphs however, we began to hear a different construction of the purpose of the activity. The criteria some children used for choosing their graphs tended to be aesthetic rather than mathematical. Their preference was for graphs which looked complex and/or unusual. Questions about the meaning of their graphs were often met with incomprehension. It began to emerge that the children did not see graphs as meaningful, or as ways of communicating information. Their construction of the purpose of graphs, based on their previous experiences within school, was that graphs were essentially decorative and used to brighten up classroom displays.

One way of looking at this behaviour is to see it as analogous to the activity described as 'emergent writing'. Young children typically begin to imitate the behaviour of adult writing long before they develop the skills required for 'real' writing. In doing so, they imitate both the form and the purpose of the activity. They don't just write, they write letters, shopping lists and menus. By engaging in this activity, they learn important lessons about the purposes of writing. I would like to describe the activity many children engaged in with the spreadsheet as 'emergent graphing'. The power of the technology allowed them to play at producing the sorts of graphs they had seen in the adult world. Taking this view of the children's behaviour had an important effect in shaping our responses to them. The strategy we decided to adopt was to accept these graphs, and to encourage children to work with them in ways that we worked with other graphs, for example by reading back information which they contained. Alongside this, we tried to design activities in which children produced and worked with graphs – and importantly in which they saw us as teachers working with graphs – in more directed ways. Gradually, we felt that the children's understanding of the purpose of graphing developed as they enlarged their range of skills in using them (Ainley, 1995; Pratt, 1995).

What do we mean by the 'real world'?

Problems in using 'real world' contexts

So far I have tried to make the case that attempts to teach mathematics in primary schools in ways which support children in applying mathematical knowledge through the use of real world contexts are problematic in a number of ways:

1. the examples chosen may not relate to the everyday lives and concerns of children;
2. word problems often have a context but no purpose, as mathematics is not used in the same ways as it would actually be in real life; and
3. the purposes of mathematical knowledge are not clear to children, and so they may make different constructions of the purposes of mathematical activities from those which are intended by their teachers.

Rather than a move towards more emphasis on fluency in calculation *per se*, which seems to underlie current government-led initiatives in the UK, there seems to me to be a need to re-think how mathematics is taught in primary schools in a way which takes account of the need to appreciate the purposes and power of mathematical ideas. An area of research in mathematics education which offers a different perspective on the difficulties of applying mathematical knowledge is the exploration of the uses of mathematics in different areas of everyday life and employment (see, for example, Lave, 1988; Nunes, Schliemann and Carraher, 1993; Schliemann, 1995). Much of this research indicates that the mathematical techniques taught in school are often not used in out-of-school contexts such as market trading, but are replaced by informal methods, closely tailored to the needs of the situation.

An apprenticeship model

An important outcome of this research has been the recognition that, far from being an inferior form of mathematical activity, 'street mathematics' has characteristics which may be of value in formal education. On this basis, a number of developments have explored ways of bringing features of street mathematics into the classroom via 'naturally occurring or meaningfully imagined situations' (Nunes, Schliemann and Carraher, 1993). One feature of street mathematics which has been discussed by a number of researchers as potentially transferable to the classroom is the notion of an apprenticeship model of teaching and learning (see, for example, Lave, 1988; Masingila, 1993). In analysing the advantages of an apprenticeship model, Masingila identifies three key features:

> (a) an apprenticeship model enables mathematical knowledge to be developed within a context, (b) cognitive development can occur as students work cooperatively with their teacher, and (c) a mathematics culture is developed within the classroom and students are initiated into this mathematics community.   (Masingila, 1993: 21)

This analysis overlooks a crucial difference between the classroom and out-of-school contexts, namely that of purpose. When an apprentice learns carpet laying, fishing or carpentry by working alongside a master, both are essentially engaged in the *same* purposeful task, although they may perform different aspects of it. The master's agenda includes initiating the apprentice, and the apprentice knows that he or she is there to learn, but overlaying this is the value and purpose of the task which is being performed. Master and apprentice share an understanding of the overall task, and the purpose for the individual skills and techniques that are require to complete it. For both of them, there is a clear pay-off in performing the task well.

In the classroom, even if situations can be created where children's interest is engaged in purposeful or meaningfully imagined tasks, and in which they can work cooperatively with their teacher, the purposes of the tasks of master and apprentices will not be the same. The teacher's purpose is not to create the computer program, build a puppet theatre, explore the mathematics within an investigation or to win the game; it is to teach. What is more, both teacher and pupils know this, and any pretence on the teacher's part that things are otherwise will be recognized as such. Thus, even though the apprenticeship model offers much that is of value in thinking about creating meaningful mathematical experiences in the classroom, I feel it is important to be realistic about its limitations.

Situated cognition

Lave's (1988) notion of learning as *situated* within a particular context offers a useful framework within which to explore aspects of children's behaviour in mathematics classrooms. Lave sees the context in which learning takes place as shaping the cognition, whilst at the same time being shaped, in the learner's perception, by the cognition. This notion of situated cognition has proved valuable in providing ways of looking at cognition in 'out-of-school' contexts. As illustrated earlier, I believe that there is also a value in turning the focus back into the classroom, and looking at school mathematics as situated within the complex environment of the classroom. In particular, I see the individual's ways of constructing purpose within an activity as a key feature of the context. The classroom is, to a considerable extent, the 'real world' of young children.

What is 'real' mathematics

In this discussion it is difficult to avoid the expressions 'real', 'reality' and 'real world'. I find these words extremely problematic. I was interested to see that within the government's new initiative for primary schools, the National Numeracy Strategy, the framework which gives the details of what pupils 'should be taught' always refers to *solving problems involving numbers in 'real life'* with the term 'real life' in quotation marks. However, when the examples given in this section include the following:

> A beetle has 6 legs. How many legs have 9 beetles?
> > (Department for Education and Employment, 1999)

the qualification on reality is perhaps advisable. (I am, incidentally, at somewhat of a loss as to how the interpret the distinction made within the same document between 'real life' problems and 'problems involving money and measures and time'.)

However, although problematic, I find these terms unavoidable, and so I would like to suggest ways in which I feel they can be used appropriately in relation to primary school mathematics. First I want to detach the notion of *reality* from contexts, and attach it instead to the perceptions of individuals. So, a problem involving the lengths of curtains in relation to particular windows is a *real* context for me as an adult with an interest in interior decorating, but is not real for most primary school children, or for a colleague who finds the subject of curtains unexciting.

Secondly, I want to detach 'real' from 'real world' or 'real life'. The quality of an individual's engagement with a problem which makes it 'real' for them does not lie solely in its utility or application, nor in its physical existence. For young children, the boundaries between fact and fantasy are often drawn differently from those of adults, but even adults can become highly engaged with problems which are set in fantasy contexts, such as calculating the height of a giant when given his or her hand measurements.

Finally, I want to extend the notion of 'real-ness' being a quality of how an individual perceives and engages with a problem and detach 'real' from the opposite of 'abstract'. Abstract problems can be very real in terms of the interest and engagement they arouse. The development of mathematics has been driven by the need to solve problems, both practical and abstract, and by the pure joy of exploration. I do not believe that we have the right to deny children access to huge areas of mathematical understanding, history, culture and pleasure by making the enormously arrogant assumption on their behalf that only what belongs to the 'real world' can be interesting.

A different perspective on mathematical activity

Research into children's perceptions of the purposes of teachers' questions (Ainley, 1988) led to my first notion of the ways in which children's experience of mathematical activity are shaped by the school context. It seems to me now that the same shift in perspective may offer an alternative account of why attempts to contextualize mathematics in the classroom are often ineffective. If, as my research indicated, children construct the majority of teachers' spoken questions as designed to test their understanding, it seems likely that they may interpret written questions, such as word problems, in the same way, regardless of the purposes for which teachers use them. Indeed, there seems to be a number of rather different purposes which teachers or curriculum developers may have in mind when setting mathematical ideas and techniques in context. Three possibilities are:

1. to support children's understanding of the mathematics;
2. to support children in transferring their knowledge to situations outside the classroom by showing them what it is useful for; and
3. to test the children's understanding by requiring them to apply their knowledge.

All three of these purposes can be constructed from typical text materials available in primary schools, and from the (often very similar) examples which teachers themselves invent. In many textbooks, word problems frequently form the last section on the page, following more straightforward examples of the 'sums' on their own. As the contents of the page generally progress in difficulty, it is natural to see this last section as the most difficult, designed to extend your thinking, or to catch you out, depending on your point of view. Contextualized problems are sometimes, but less often, used at the beginning of a new topic, where they might more easily be seen as designed to help children's understanding of the mathematics.

Children's perceptions of contextualized problems
I conjecture that many children will construct the use of contextualized problems in school mathematics as a hurdle to be overcome, rather than as an aid to their learning. The problems are there to make it more difficult to recognize the calculation which has to be carried out to arrive at the right answer, which is, after all, what the school game is all about. If children construct the purpose of the activity in this way, then a sensible strategy to adopt is to pay no attention to the context, which may distract from this goal. It may be that children are not *unable* to interpret word problems or to transfer mathematical knowledge from one situation to another – in the classroom situation, they simply may not see this as the purpose of the activity.

The classroom context

Children's experience of mathematics as an activity is largely situated in classrooms, and shaped by their perceptions of the purposes of schooling. I believe that the underlying reason why most attempts to contextualize mathematics fail to enable children to apply their knowledge in other situations is because of a failure to pay attention to how the *purposes* of mathematical activity are understood by the participants. Teachers and curriculum developers may use 'real world' contexts with the purpose of showing pupils how a particular piece of mathematics can be useful, but if children construct the purpose of the activity – and indeed of all school mathematics – as 'getting the right answers', they will be unable to appreciate what the teacher's purpose is. Indeed, they may fail to appreciate the more fundamental idea that mathematical knowledge is useful, because the classroom context shapes their perceptions of mathematical activity so strongly. This points to the necessity to change that classroom context in order to allow children a different perspective.

The role of purpose

Motivation and purpose

I see the notion of *purpose* as central both to interpreting mathematical activity in the classroom, and to the quality of children's mathematical thinking. For me, the notion of purpose is clearly distinct from that of motivation. Children may be motivated by their enjoyment in carrying out a task, or by the novelty of a situation, but still see little purpose in what they are doing. However, the difference in the quality of attention which comes from engaging in a purposeful task is very marked.

Purposeful mathematical tasks

I have been able to experience the results of children engaged in purposeful mathematical activity in my own research on the use of computers in the learning and teaching of mathematics. Within the Primary Laptop Project, in which children and teachers are able to have regular access to a range of mathematical software, the design of purposeful tasks has become a major focus of research. Initially, we aimed for tasks that had a clear purpose within the context of the classroom. Often these involved some aspect of design, within which children could be given the freedom to explore and make decisions, and which the children themselves saw as purposeful. However, it has become apparent that these conditions are not sufficient to produce activities in which children will also engage with the mathematical ideas which are part of *our* purpose for the activities. We have come to distinguish the overt purpose of the activity which engages the children's interest (e.g. solving a problem, designing an efficient spinner or investigating the dimensions of wheels) from the *utility* of the mathematical ideas used within it (Ainley, in preparation). Thus, we have designed activities within which children will come across the need to use particular mathematical ideas, giving them the opportunity not only to learn some mathematics, but also to learn how that mathematical idea can be used, and the power that it may have. I offer two brief examples here which I hope will serve to illustrate the distinction.

Example 1: The 'helicopter'

One activity we have used with many groups of children involves trying to design a good paper 'helicopter' (aspects of this activity are discussed in Pratt, 1995). Children needed to test their designs by timing how long the helicopter flew, but quickly realized that their timings were inaccurate. Within the activity we were able to offer them the facility on the spreadsheet to find the (mean) average of a set of results as a way of balancing out the inaccuracies of their measurements. At this point the children used the computer to generate the average value which they then used to plot a graph. They did not, at this stage, learn how to calculate the average, but they did learn about the way in which this value is used as a measure of central tendency, and about how and when it can be applied to solve real problems. Failure to appreciate this aspect of the use of the mean has been identified as a significant problem in statistical education (Konold et al., 1997) The children were also sufficiently curious about how the computer did the calculation to make teaching them the procedure relatively simple. This contrasts strongly with more traditional approaches to teaching 'average', in which the calculation procedure is taught in the abstract, or in contexts which do not necessarily illuminate its purpose.

Example 2: Maximization

A second example comes from an activity involving the maximization of the area of a rectangular sheep pen (Ainley, 1996). Within this activity children made use of a graph of their results to try to identify the maximum value, and then translated their informal method for calculating the dimensions of the pen into an algebra-like spreadsheet formula to generate more (and more accurate) results. These in turn produced a more useful graph. The children's attention was primarily on solving the problem, which, despite its rather contrived setting, became real for them by being sufficiently intriguing. They are able to appreciate the utility of both the graph and the formula which would allow them to generate data which would draw a 'better' graph.

Conclusion

I believe that appreciating the utility of a concept or procedure through being able to apply it in a purposeful context is an extremely powerful way of learning mathematics. The quality of children's work, and the mathematical levels that we have been able to reach within the Primary Laptop Project, using activities which have been designed in this way, strongly support this view. Moreover, it seems that children who learn about the utility of mathematical ideas in this way, also have the opportunity to learn that mathematics is useful, not only in the adult world, but in their world as well.

7 Facts and Fantasies: What Mathematics Should Our Children Learn?

Celia Hoyles and Richard Noss
Mathematical Sciences Group, Institute of Education, University of London

Introduction

In the *Times Educational Supplement* (28 May 1999) is a report of a Department for Education and Employment (DfEE) initiative to improve 'numeracy'; it is, believe it or not, to base mathematics lessons on the playing of something called 'fantasy football'. The intention, we assume, is to make an attempt to connect the culture of (some) children with mathematics, to try to motivate them to do some mathematics by introducing it in a context they care about. However, we are certain that this idea will fail. Children dislike being patronized, they know only too well what is really required of school mathematics and some will want to know whether the mathematics classes of Winchester and Westminster will be similarly preoccupied. There is too, a real danger that the solution of any problem in fantasy football will require only knowledge of football, with no need for mathematical thinking and reasoning at anything but a superficial level. Clearly, in the hands of enthusiastic teachers and children who share this enthusiasm, we can imagine some success in this attempt to render mathematics more understandable and interesting. But not at the expense of *mathematical* goals for learning.

Perceptions of mathematics

In recent times, mathematics has become increasingly disconnected from the cultural preoccupations of ordinary people. Its image is one of fragmentation and disconnection, although in reality (and from the mathematician's perspective) it has never been more connected. Similarly, its application to fields as diverse as neurobiology or economics are testament to its practical orientation, and the astonishing growth in the application of even the most rarefied topics (such as topology) is truly breathtaking. All the stranger, then, that there is in the UK an increasing identification in popular culture of mathematics with basic arithmetic or 'numeracy' which makes it ever harder for children to gain a picture of what mathematics is about, or begin to appreciate the power of mathematical reasoning and deduction. Even the best students are confused. In a recent study we undertook of undergraduates in one of the country's major research mathematics departments, we encountered more than one who could not even imagine why a mathematician might want to prove a result (Hoyles, Newman and Noss, submitted article).

Connecting mathematics with culture

We *do* need to find ways to connect mathematics with the broader culture. We need to find ways to break down the barriers between mathematics and art, music, humanities and the social sciences, as well as, of course, science and technology. We need to find entry points into the preoccupations and aspirations of children in ways that respect the integrity of their interests rather than patronizing and inevitably disappointing them. Most importantly, we need to introduce ways to make these connections by ensuring that the solutions of problems given to our students *need* the use of mathematics, that children do have a chance to make choices of strategy for themselves and learn to reflect upon and debug them. We would like to encourage an appreciation that solving problems in and with mathematics is not a matter of routine or factual recall – although these might play a part. We had better help children (and their teachers) to see that fun can be difficult too, that motivation doesn't always have to come dressed up as something else, and that there is satisfaction and even joy to be found in doing mathematics.

Non-trivial pursuits

Mathematics and the school curriculum

Our starting point is essentially epistemological – it concerns the kinds of knowledge we believe to be fundamental. We should admit, however, that many policy-makers and others simply do not see things this way. Recent policy documents have, for example, taken the fundamental challenges of the new millennium as being concerned with *how* to teach rather than what to teach. In so far as recent policy initiatives have tackled epistemological questions, they have set a course 180 degrees in the opposite direction to that which we propose. This direction takes us into the well-charted waters of basic arithmetic, and is busily engaged in systematically stripping the mathematics curricula at all levels of precisely the kinds of mathematics which we believe is needed now and will be needed still more in the future. (This process is hardly new – see Dowling and Noss, 1989, for a relatively early critique.) Of course, what is left is elementary and essentially 'covered' in the primary school. This leads some to question the central place of mathematics as a core subject in the curriculum. If school mathematics is indeed trivial and fragmented, boring, largely misunderstood and irrelevant, why should so many students be subjected to it for so long? If there is no evidence that mathematics provides broad cognitive 'training' (and there isn't), why should we teach it? If the school mathematics curriculum consists of routines that are anachronistic and irrelevant, wouldn't the time be better spent studying something else? Viewed like this, the case of those who want to remove mathematics from the compulsory curriculum seems irrefutable – much of what passes in the UK for the 'National' Curriculum in mathematics cannot be defended as a basis for learning in the new millennium.

Readers will not be surprised to learn that we think this case is fatally flawed. We believe that mathematics is more relevant now than at any time in the history of compulsory education, but this relevance cannot be taken for granted. It is mathematics that is powerful and crucial for future citizens, not the latest version of the curriculum. If the *knowledge* presumed by our curricula doesn't change, or worse, if we 'return to basics' by widening still further the gap between what we teach and what children need, then we concede to the critics – let us save children from it.

It is commonplace to encounter polemics arguing for 'traditional' school mathematics, a small body of content and skills that is fixed, known and must be delivered. In a surprisingly short time, it has become the established orthodoxy of English curricula in mathematics (and more generally). For most, the study of mathematics now comprises elementary number work, a little algebra, shape and space (a euphemism for geometry) and some 'data handling' as statistics is quaintly called. Yet we know that simply confining mathematics to these areas will inevitably fail to deliver competence, *even within these limited confines*. The explanation is simple. This school mathematics only focuses on fragments of content and skill while mathematical meaning is engendered by building connections *across* topics, exploring patterns *among* signs, symbols and representations, making conjectures, proving and explaining them by reference to *different* modes of representation. To take just one example, fluency in algebra is certainly required for competence in mathematics, but so too is flexibility in thinking about geometric structures and more particularly seeing the connections between these two modes (see Noss, Healy and Hoyles, 1997).

The centrality of mathematics

In case we are misunderstood, we should emphasize that we believe that mathematical thinking must be built on knowledge. However, facts or, in their latest incarnation which we shall discuss later, 'information', are not enough. Far too many people whose lives – whether they like it or not – have been revolutionized by mathematics, imagine that its high point is long division.

To engage students and to warrant its central place in the school curriculum, mathematics needs to be seen as a living, changing discipline. Mathematics has a role beyond the basic functionality associated with numeracy and simple algebra: as a powerful language for building, systematizing and sharing knowledge. Mathematics underpins all of the sciences. Moreover, as Kaput and Roschelle argued:

> We want to lead students towards understandings of the larger mathe-
> matics of change and variation that includes dynamical systems because
> this relatively new mathematical form, with roots in Poincaré's work at
> the end of the previous century, is revolutionizing many sciences ... .
> (Kaput and Roschelle, 1999: 67)

Mathematics is increasingly adding new dimensions to the interpretation
of the social sciences as well. As the Millennium Mathematics Project[1]
puts it:

> Mathematics supports the fabric of modern life – our financial systems
> and medical services, our communication networks, our entertainment
> and leisure activities ... and is vital to the continuing economic health
> of society.

But is this merely rhetoric? Does the ubiquity of mathematics consump-
tion imply a need for anybody except its producers to understand what
they are doing? Is it important that all should be aware of this 'real' mathematics? Is it not, perhaps, better that the majority are simply trained in
numeracy? Such arguments between traditional and 'new' mathematics
tend to intensify when there is some sort of crisis in social or economic
spheres – although the direction of these is by no means automatic: at the
moment, much of Asia is gripped by a 'creativity crisis' which involves
trying to encourage students to think for themselves instead of learning
by rote. (See Lin and Tsao, 1999; Lew, 1999.)

   In parts of the UK, of course, the swing is in the other direction, under
cover of the fact that UK students did not perform well in international
comparisons of responses in number and algebra (see, for example, Keys,
Harris and Fernandes, 1996), and the decline in the number of mathematics graduates entering teaching. (It is worth noting that UK students
came at or near the top of the Third International Mathematics and Science
Study (TIMSS) tables in problem-solving and geometry, an inconvenience
which has not troubled policy-makers to any great extent.)

   As the lines of definition around school mathematics are drawn ever
tighter, the case of those who believe that mathematics is a pointless
endeavour for most is strengthened – as we argued above, their definition

of mathematical activity renders their conclusions inevitable. Traditional school mathematics neither warrants the time it takes in the curriculum nor the outcomes it achieves in terms of student learning. If mathematics is reduced to simple arithmetic, then most children should be able to learn what they need by the time they enter secondary school. In which case, mathematics can be dispensed with, and with it, any serious appreciation of physics, the principles of engineering, or anything other than the most descriptive and superficial analyses in the social sciences. No matter, there is no shortage of those who will accommodate this sea change in culture (a recent advertisement for a book has appeared on our desk entitled *Statistics without Mathematics* – a symptom of an increasingly widespread disease).

The interpretive power of mathematics

We are not arguing that mathematics is sufficient for understanding, say, social science, but we are arguing that it is necessary. In fact, we can only agree with the following observation, made nearly a century ago:

> Mathematical expressions have, however, their special tendencies to pervert thought: the definiteness may be spurious, existing in the equations but not in the phenomena to be described; the brevity may be due to the omission of the more important things, simply because they cannot be mathematized Richardson, L.F. (1919) *Mathematical Psychology of War.* (Quoted in Hunt and Neunzert, 1994: 269)

Our argument is not that the world can only be understood through mathematics; it is that mathematics should be an essential tool for understanding it and the phenomena that can be understood mathematically are growing with leading-edge developments in the discipline. Unless some cultural change occurs in education and outside, more and more of the world will be less and less understandable to more and more people. Understanding the world demands intuition, engagement, morality and a range of intellectual 'skills' which lie strictly outside the domain of mathematics. However, to interpret the patterns of the world demands that these patterns are analysed, and this analysis requires the kinds of mathematical thinking we have outlined. More importantly, it necessitates an awareness that these models exist and can be analysed.

Understanding systems: the real potential of digital technologies

Modelling 'chaotic' phenomena

A short time ago, when we and most readers of this chapter were at school, the geometry of a leaf defied mathematical description. We could accept that its chemical composition could be described mathematically, that the distribution of leaves might be amenable to statistical analysis, that its rate of growth might be concisely captured by one or more differential equations. But not its shape.

Now, just a few decades later, we take for granted that the geometry of leaves, as much as bolts of lightening or 'random' fluctuations on the stock market or weather systems, can be modelled mathematically. It is almost obligatory for coffee tables to be adorned by the latest book on complexity or chaos, and its vocabulary has entered into popular culture and linguistic convention (in the process, of course, some of the essential meaning of both has been lost).

We cannot take for granted that this new knowledge, and its spread within the culture, is an unquestionably positive event in the history of science. It might be argued that some of this knowledge is being or will be put to use in ways which do not benefit our societies. Or one may adopt a position that knowledge, *per se*, is neutral, and that any scientific advance which adds to that knowledge must be greeted with approbation. This question is the tip of an ideological iceberg, and we do not choose to explore it here. Instead we ask a much simpler question whose relevance will emerge shortly: what was the role of digital technologies in these developments?

Our answer will suppress all technical detail. The mathematical foundation of 'chaos' theory was laid a century ago, and it is commonplace to observe that its implications had to wait for the advent of cheap, ubiquitous and powerful computing technology. There is no doubt that the demanding use of technology which allowed a whole new class of phenomena to be mathematized, contributed to a wave of interest among mathematicians, as well as economists, biologists and others who took up the ideas. These fields now represent a leading edge of the research in chaos. As far as the broader culture is concerned, there is no question that the stunning computer-generated 'fractals' (the geometrical face of chaotic behaviour), pointing so vividly to the increasingly fuzzy boundaries between mathematics and art, geometry and design, have played a central role in the popularization of the idea of chaos.

Computer programming in mathematics education

Changes in mathematics are dialectically linked to advances in technology and this reciprocity has rendered the discipline more powerful and play-ful, more integrative across disciplines and modes of thought. Digital technologies have engendered a hitherto unthinkable degree of engage-ment with mathematical objects and relationships. From an educational point of view, more students can now be involved in mathematical activity, as long as we redefine what this means in an honest way. In fact, this *was* the trend in the use of computers in schools in the mid 1980s. A UK govern-ment report on school mathematics (Department of Education and Science, 1985) advised that, in order to use computers as a powerful means of doing mathematics, children will need to program the machines, and that 'if programming is not taught elsewhere, it should be included in mathe-matics lessons' (Department of Education and Science, 1985: 35). The link between programming and mathematics education which the report sought to establish was in precisely the right direction: constructing models and taking them apart.

How quickly times change. This move has been swept aside in the tide of information which now threatens to engulf *all* use of digital technologies in an educational context. The contribution of programs is precisely the building of *mechanisms*, the description of how things *work*. This is what we mean when we argue for models, not some arcane and impenetrable course in a programming language, but the creation of ways to make workings visible. Here we return to nonlinear dynamics or chaos. For at no point in the astonishing explosion of mathematical knowledge has *information* been crucial, except in trivial ways. Information technology (IT) (or as it is now more politically correct to call it information and communications technology (ICT)) did not provide information except in the trivial sense. The scientific breakthroughs, and their applications in diverse fields as well as the broader culture, owed nothing to the gathering or communication of information *per se*, and everything to the technology's affordance in supporting visualization, classification and the illumination of *structure*.

Knowledge beyond ICT

'The learning society', as well as other Good Things is supposed to rely heavily on IT, disseminated along the *information* superhighway. Information is important; it is central to learning. Without information, factual knowledge, there can be no learning. Yet there is more to knowledge than information. The major advances of scientific (and artistic and humanistic) thought are seldom *about* information. To use digital technologies primarily as a means to search for and communicate information is to miss a massive opportunity to bring about cultural change of the kind we need.

It has become commonplace to elaborate a kind of technological utopianism, in which the mere presence of technology is guaranteed to give rise to educational opportunity, enhanced motivation and increased learning in schools and outside. We will not waste time on this ubiquitous and thoroughly unhelpful trend, which has reached its apogee in some recent government pronouncements (but see Buckingham, 1999, for a reasoned critique). However, there are more sophisticated visions of technology in which the presence of technology itself is acknowledged as a necessary but insufficient ingredient. In this scenario, access to huge swathes of information is taken for granted, and the educational potential lies in giving people the skills to sift and sort it. While this is an improvement on the former view, this stance similarly places its emphasis on the need to gain information, and as we shall see, necessarily paints a very partial picture of the reality of the kinds of knowledge the twenty-first century will require.

The knowledge we need now

What then, is this knowledge? The mathematics education that will be needed for the future by the 'educated person', by the employee in an environment of constantly developing technology was the topic of a recent book edited by Hoyles, Morgan and Woodhouse (1999). The chapters written by a wide variety of stakeholders from industry, mathematics, commerce and education present a remarkably convergent vision of a mathematics curriculum that is needed – one built around the construction and interpretation of quantitative models.

In a recent paper, we argued that the key necessity for the new millennium was for people to understand the systems they use:

> The massive computerization of systems will, to a greater or lesser degree, herald new kinds of craft and expertise. It will mean that more and more people will need to modify and rebuild systems with their own variables and parameters, not just plug in values to someone else's. It will mean that the distinction between domain specific knowledge of mathematical facts and generalizable skills will become increasingly obsolete. And, for our teaching of numeracies, it will involve constructing new educational cultures in which individuals have the means to make sense of the models, and the means to express them algebraically, geometrically and computationally. New cultures of work are redefining the boundaries of what needs to be understood as a whole, rather than as isolated skills ... .
>
> Increasingly, not only scientists and social scientists, but technicians, clerks and health workers, will need to understand those basic principles, they will need to sort out what has gone wrong, what mathematical knowledge has been buried invisibly beneath the surface of their computers, and how to dig it out. As the demands of workplace practices point beyond mere pattern recognition, and beyond that which can be grasped by any one individual – however well educated – solutions to problems will need to draw on precisely the kind of mathematization which is embodied in computational models. People will need to represent to themselves what has happened, particularly whenever the activities in which they are involved become in some way non-routine.
>
> (Noss, 1997: 17–18)

The mathematical base of complex systems

Before we consider the implications of this view, we wish to add something to our analysis. We will inevitably come to rely on highly complex systems, in which failure to understand them may have dire consequences. But isn't this simply apocalyptic? Society is already complex, and we have managed to survive somehow. Perhaps so, but there is a new factor. The complexity of the system is now built on mathematical principles. The computers are, increasingly, not just tools for implementing the system – they *are* the system. In such a scenario, therefore, any model of the system has to involve a mathematical representation which must be related formally to the structures on which the system was designed. Whereas one might easily argue that the social and scientific systems of the previous two millennia could be – for the most part – described and interpreted without formal mathematics, this will simply not be an option in the third millennium. The models we need will have to capture the dynamics of social and scientific systems, and they will need to be interpretable by the many, not just by the few. Our educational priorities should, therefore, be geared to helping individuals to make sense of models in appropriate kinds of description languages. This inevitably will lead to a widening of mathematical forms of expression beyond those tried and tested in the past.

Let us state our thesis succinctly. People will need to know how to understand relationships between phenomena; they will need to recognize and explain pattern; and they will need to interpret – and make for themselves – conceptual models of phenomena and be able to make deductions and predictions on the basis of these. They will need, in short, to have some induction into the science of pattern, a science which usually goes under the name of mathematics.

New knowledge in practice

In this section, we present some evidence from our recent studies of mathematics of the workplace in order to contextualize the rift between traditional and mathematical perspectives and elaborate our contention of the importance of mathematical modelling.

'Basic' skills

Given that there are curriculum reforms which purportedly attempt to make mathematics more applicable to the contexts in which it will later be applied, a plausible hypothesis is that young people should be better prepared to tackle the mathematical problems and tasks found in working and everyday life. However, this area has remained virtually unresearched in the UK for the last 15 years, and what little research there has been has not ventured far from the utilitarian approach used in the Cockcroft studies (1982). For example, a recent five-page report commissioned by the School Curriculum and Assessment Authority (SCAA) (1997) includes a survey of employers' and employees' use of mathematics, defined by a tick list of mathematics curriculum topics. From these and other data, the researchers concluded that employers were mainly concerned with employees' numeracy and estimation skills, and their over-reliance on calculators. Of course. One glance at the tick list should be sufficient to conclude that this 'research' would reach this finding. The tautological knot has been tied – once mathematics is defined as basic numeracy, it is inevitable, as we have argued, to conclude that employees need only numeracy, and that they are not terribly good even at that.

Researching the mathematics in skilled work

In fact, we have believed for some time that finding out what employees actually *do* mathematically in work merits serious research. So we set out[2] to analyse the authentic mathematics of highly skilled professional groups (bankers, nurses and pilots) and evaluate the extent to which their activity possessed a mathematical dimension. Unlike the SCAA approach, this mathematics was not predefined and constrained by the specifications of the school curriculum. Rather we saw workplace mathematical activity as comprising social as well as mental or individual skills – an ability to communicate about quantities and the relationships between them, and to explain and reason about these relationships in the work context using the representational resources available. These aims meant that we had to adopt a methodology which involved immersion in the practice, seeing and analysing what actually happened and not simply asking a few individuals what they thought they did. (See also Hall, 1999, who adopted a similar methodology.)

Outcomes

Overall, our work has suggested that the analysis of mathematics at work presents a surprisingly complex picture. It is different from mathematics as traditionally conceived in educational settings. Rather than striving towards consistency and generality, mathematical problem-solving at work is characterized by pragmatic concerns and is geared towards solving particular problems. For optimal efficiency, occupational or professional concerns are considered in tandem with mathematical ones. Moreover, people develop strategies using available features of their environment (including their colleagues), exploiting local regularities where possible in efforts to carry out their work quickly and efficiently. Most crucially, the mathematical models that underpin their practice are rarely those predicted by a school mathematics curriculum. Yet an appreciation of the significant variables in these models, an understanding as to why these variables are important, and feeling empowered to act on data from the models are all crucial.

An example: investment banking[3]

Our early work in this field involved a major multi-national investment bank. They told us that many of their employees (secretaries, technicians as well as some 'bankers') had little mathematical appreciation of the models underpinning the financial instruments they were using on a daily basis – not surprisingly given their sophistication. They found difficulty in spotting mistakes and recognizing the limitations of the models, with the result that the bank was losing money. Mathematics provided the infrastructure of the banking operation, but was largely taken for granted or ignored in pursuit of banking objectives. However at times of conflict – and there is nothing so conflictual for a bank as losing money! – the tools became noticed, the implicit shifted to the explicit. Explanations needed to be found and communicated. The situation described by the bank highlighted the problematic relationship between using a mathematical tool and understanding its essence.

Here was a classic situation. How could we assist people to appropriate the mathematics they used on a daily basis? Our first step was to immerse ourselves as far as possible in the practice of banking, to seek to understand the essence of financial mathematics by talking to a wide range of employees, watching them at work, interviewing them *in situ* and reading the literature on the mathematics of finance, trying to make sense of the new language we found there – every field has its own language and banking is certainly no exception. Our struggle was to keep the connection of mathematics with banking, so that meanings from one domain could feed into the other and vice-versa. This approach was completely novel to our bank employees. On the one hand, as far as we could tell, financial mathematics courses simply taught the relevant mathematical tools as a system separated from banking practice leaving frustration in their wake. On the other hand, the books we read left most of the mathematical work invisible; it was bypassed with deliberately opaque phrases such as 'it can be shown' or 'this can be proved mathematically'. Such devices inevitably leave the reader in a powerless state – unless they have the resources to fill in the gaps in the text which, as we can now testify, was by no means a trivial task.

One particular incident will serve to illustrate the problem. Percentages are part of the everyday discourse of the bank, at the heart of the assessment of profit and loss and the basis on which deals are made. Yet we were struck by some surprising mythologies which surrounded this notion, which led us to ask number of bank employees the following question (in a rather casual way – we had misgivings, as we wondered whether it was insultingly simple):

If you take £100, and add 8%, you get £108. What happens if you take 8% off the answer?

Most knew that the answer was not £100, and were able to work out the answer. But not all. Sally, for example, was a senior administrative assistant, someone who was responsible for the coordination and oversight of a substantial department. She told us:

> I know the answer's not £100. I've always wondered why. I just assumed it's because numbers are funny!

Sally's confusion (and 'explanation') is not so far-fetched. Numbers are funny … unless one 'understands' what is happening. But what does understanding mean? We wondered how to help Sally; she became an early litmus test we applied when designing our approach to pedagogical intervention. We know that difficulties with percentages are widespread and that many strategies are adopted to cope with different types of questions – although in school, rule-driven methods tend to come to predominate. But here we have a situation where dealing with percentages was part of working practice. We conjectured that the very familiarity of percentages may be such that they were never explicitly the object of reflection; the relations inherent in the percentage idea were, in contrast to school mathematics, far less significant than the comparisons between different percentage rates. However, Sally had no model of what percentages were all about – re-teaching rules would not help. She needed to build and debug models of the financial systems with which she worked, all of which involved percentages.

So, more generally, our objective had to be to find ways in which our students could abstract relationships *within* (rather than away from) their working practices – or at least situations which mirrored these practices. Our challenge was to find ways of encouraging the bankers to think about their familiar practices in ways which included the mathematical, rather than by replacing them by 'mathematics'.

There were difficulties associated with this approach when we tried to put it into operation. The first was epistemological: how far could we go? To what extent could we provide a new ontology for the bankers? The second difficulty was pedagogical. If we attempted to get at the underlying mathematical ideas, we would need rigour. Yet unification and rigour are mathematical priorities, not those of banking practice. Worse still, mathematical rigour is pregnant with meaning, but only for those who are already inducted into its discourse.

Our challenge was to design an environment which afforded rigour with meaning, ways of expressing relationships mathematically without the presupposition that students already knew what we were trying to teach. We decided to adopt the same approach as that which we had tried and tested with children, to open a window for the bank employees onto mathematical ideas through helping them to build and debug models through programming.

This was an ideal setting to test out our theoretical and empirical approach, but one that was challenging in its unfamiliarity and high stakes. First, we constructed our own computer models of a range of simplified financial situations. Building models helped us to connect our mathematics to banking, and to sort out what might be the big issues from a mathematical point of view. We trusted that the same process of model building would work in the other direction, connecting for our banker-students their knowledge of banking to mathematics.

Our approach was to view all financial instruments in terms of what we viewed as their common mathematical structure, so that different financial instruments could be compared, contrasted and modelled. We planned to immerse students in a programming environment not as a quick way to represent and manipulate data but rather as a means for building representations of relationships symbolically and graphically.

Alongside our intention to make mathematics more visible for our students, we wanted our students to make the practice of banking more visible for us. Thus, our students were co-designers; we wanted to learn (and incorporate into subsequent versions of our materials) how a more systematic, mathematical, view of the banking world could assist in understanding banking practice. We wanted examples from our students which they could work on and explore in the context of their working practices, and from which we could then learn.

Pedagogically, our approach was broadly constructionist (Harel and Papert, 1991). We structured our activities around starting points meaningful to the participants, but which could be seen as jumping-off points for broader investigation and exploration of banking. We put students in the position of constructing their own simplified but nonetheless powerful models on the computer. For many, it was the first time they had produced a model of anything, despite being consumers of hundreds of different models developed by unseen programmers every day. We tried to incorporate a range of striking examples and intriguing questions. Why should we not expect interest rates to move by full percentage points in 1995 while this was the norm at the turn of the century? What happens to an investment as the frequency of compound interest payments is increased, and why? What is the difference between simple interest and discount instruments? Model the situation for yourself and see if the model helps – and if it doesn't, build a new one.

We re-learned an important insight – the extent to which we can understand and teach a new idea is precisely the extent to which we can build a model – a program to express it. In a modest way, we showed to ourselves (and we hope, to our students) that building a model of how something works is a marvellous way to understand it (not the only one!), a lesson which most of us have forgotten at about the same time as we stopped building Lego toys. And it is a lesson which points to a broader conclusion, in which digital technologies might provide just the right cohesive material for building a more rational, useful and understandable mathematics.

Computers connecting cultures

Our premise is that in order not to be disempowered either as citizens or as employees, individuals will need more and more powerful mathematics, and that if nations are to develop culturally and economically their populations will need to become more not less sophisticated mathematically. The Chief Executive of 'our' bank went so far as to point to data he had collected that showed a strong correlation between the mathematical expertise of his employees and success at the bank, as measured by the salary, bonuses and promotion – a finding which neither he nor we can explain satisfactorily. This point of view has been given support by a recent study in the United States, which reported that the biggest factor in determining whether young people earned a bachelor's degree was their participation in a strong academic curriculum in high school. Moreover, a report, *Answers in the Tool Box* (Adelman, 1999), based on data from a national cohort of students who were followed from tenth grade in 1980 until roughly age 30 in 1993, found that by the age of 30, some 65 per cent of high school graduates had attended some form of post-secondary education, and 40 per cent had attended a four-year college. Of those, 63 per cent had earned a bachelor's degree. The relevance of this study is that neither race nor family income were significant predictors of whether a young person graduated from a four-year college, once other factors were taken into account. In contrast, the *level of mathematics* that students studied in high school appeared to have the strongest continuing influence on whether they earned a bachelor's degree.

> Finishing a mathematics course beyond the level of Algebra 2 more than doubles the odds that a kid will get a bachelor's degree, and that's controlling for everything else.
>
> (See http://www.edweek.org/ew/current/38grad.h18)

Communicating complexity

We cannot afford to limit the horizons of our students by giving them a reduced and trivialized mathematical education. But how can we enhance their motivation and their competence while at the same time, offering them an authentic mathematics? Every other artefact in our culture contains a system, a mathematical model wrapped into a technology; but, of course, the mathematics is invisible, the system is unreadable and the model impenetrable. Can we really exploit this technology for education? Isn't there a paradox? Surely the very point of digital technologies is (mostly) to *hide* – not make visible – the mathematics which has been frozen into it? We have argued this case in considerable detail in our book (Noss and Hoyles, 1996), and we cannot rehearse it here. Our general point in the book was summed up thus:

From the point of view of school mathematics, the computer can catalyse the opening of new entry points, particularly those from outside school. Our grounds for viewing this optimistically should be clear by now: the tendency to trivialise change … which transforms mathematical content into hierarchies and packages, the pressures to disconnect mathematics from all sources of meanings; all these mitigate against the construction of more learnable mathematics inside schools. But the computer, whether we like it or not, has become, in Papert's memorable phrase, the 'children's machine'; whether we empathize with the nihilistic culture of arcade games or not, children have appropriated them. Even though children own nothing of the huge corporate software designers, they do own a little of the culture: just enough perhaps to open a chink in the armour which protects access to the portals of the mathematics which underpins it.   (Noss and Hoyles, 1996: 251)

The development of mathematical meanings involves engaging with appropriately complex and interesting questions, as well as having the intellectual resources and tools to express the current state of one's understandings. When we focused our bankers' attention on functions and their graphical expression by constructing models, they started to build connections between their banking practice and academic mathematics. There is a generalizable lesson here: people encounter all kinds of mathematical ideas in their working lives, but they are, in general, unaware of them. Bankers, nurses and pilots are too busy doing their job to reflect on the mathematical structures which underpin the systems they use. It would be perverse to argue that they would be 'better' at their job if they understood the mathematics; in any case, most of the systems are too complex to 'understand' in any real sense. But is it too much to expect that people at work should know what makes their systems tick? Understand what its elements are? Tinker with it perhaps? Certainly, one of the key rationales for the bank's management in asking us to 'teach mathematics' was in order for employees in different sections to gain a common language. Communication of complexity seems to us a key rationale for learning mathematics.

An example: computer games

We conclude with a glimpse of our latest work, which provides something of a contrast to our bank employees – it involves children of eight years and less.[4] In this we are hoping to use a powerful cultural connection which has yet to be fully exploited for mathematical learning: that of computer games. We are building virtual worlds – we call them 'playgrounds' – based on the idea of children constructing rather than just consuming computer games. Unlike most computer games, in which the metaphors are simple, the tools immediate to provide entertainment and the systems closed, our games will be built for learning, openness and creativity. Our challenge is to build a system in which playing games and playing with games are simultaneously fun and an introduction to the rules underpinning them. We are trying to build a system for children to design games and play with their rules.

Rather than summarize these, we illustrate these possibly unfamiliar ideas with a story. Michael, an eight-year-old boy in an inner-city primary school, is playing a game which involves controlling (with a force joystick – one which pushes back!) – an object on the screen in two dimensions. As he makes it fly around the screen, he 'shoots' flowers at moving objects (the choice of flowers – thankfully not bullets – and the target objects were his own). As the flowers hit moving objects, these transform into new objects, and make appropriately ear-splitting noises. He is having fun, but it is hard to know what he might be learning – tempting even to dismiss this as just another arcade game.

He decides that it would be more fun with two players. So one of us helps him to reprogram his game to do this. Again, an observer might be forgiven for asking what he might have learned by this, as there was no explicit 'teaching' in any formal sense, just a joint negotiation of what to change and how.

Then, suddenly, Michael asks everyone watching to close their eyes – he is going to play a trick on them.

We will describe the trick in adult terms which were certainly not used by Michael. His idea was simple – he realized that if the player can move left and right as well as up and down, he or she can get 'too near' to the target. So he disabled the horizontal component of the motion, by simply removing it from the program. Simple? Perhaps. Yet none of the adults present had any idea that Michael had realized this 'simple' idea – decomposition of vectors into horizontal and vertical components has not yet found its way into the attainment targets of Key Stage 2! Yet here was an eight-year-old boy for whom such an idea (even if unarticulated) seemed perfectly natural. Why? Because he was engaged in a project which he cared about, and in which understanding the system and the mathematics which underpinned it, was important. The message is *not* that decomposition of vectors should become this or that new attainment target. It is that carefully designed digital technologies involve children naturally in mathematizing their realities. And not a fantasy football in sight.

Notes

1. The Millennium Mathematics Project is a national initiative based at Cambridge University, UK, which was launched in July 1999 with a broad goal to help people of all age and abilities share in the excitement of mathematics and understand the vital importance of its applications to science and commerce (see http://www.mmp.maths.org.uk).
2. Together with our colleague, Stefano Pozzi, and thanks to the Economic and Social Research Council, Grant No. RO22250004. The final report of the project can be found at www.ioe.ac.uk/rnoss/tmo/
3. This section is based on Noss, R. and Hoyles, C. (1996), 'The visibility of meanings: modelling the mathematics of banking'. *International Journal of Computers for Mathematical Learning*, 1, 3–31.
4. See http://www.ioe.ac.uk/playground.

Bibliography

Adelman, C. (1999), *Answers in the Tool Box. Academic Intensity, Attendance Patterns, and Bachelor's Degree Attainment*. Washington, DC: National Institute on Postsecondary Education, Libraries and Lifelong Learning.

Adult Literacy and Basic Skills Unit (ALBSU) (1987), *Literacy, Numeracy and Adults: Evidence from the National Child Development Study*. London: ALBSU.

Ainley, J. (1988), 'Perceptions of teachers' questioning styles'. In A. Borbás (ed.), *Proceedings of the Twelfth Conference of the International Group for the Psychology of Mathematics Education*. Hungary: Vesprem, I, 92–99.

Ainley, J. (1991), 'Is there any mathematics in measurement?' In D. Pimm and E. Love (eds), *Teaching and Learning School Mathematics*. London: Hodder and Stoughton, 69–76.

Ainley, J. (1995), 'Re-viewing graphing: traditional and intuitive approaches'. *For the Learning of Mathematics*, 15(2), 10–16.

Ainley, J. (1996), 'Purposeful contexts for formal notation in a spreadsheet environment'. *Journal of Mathematical Behavior*, 15(4), 405–422.

Ainley, J. (in preparation), 'Transparency in graphs and graphing tasks: an iterative design process'. *Journal of Mathematical Behavior*.

Ainley, J. and Pratt, D. (1995), 'Planning for portability'. In L. Burton and B. Jaworski (eds), *Technology and Mathematics Teaching: a bridge between teaching and learning*. Bromley: Chartwell Bratt, 435–448.

Arcavi, A. (1994), 'Symbol sense: the informal sense-making in formal mathematics'. *For the Learning of Mathematics*, 14(3), 24–35.

Ashford, S., Gray, J. and Tranmer, M. (1993), 'The introduction of GCSE exams and changes in post-16 participation'. Employment Department Research Series, Youth Cohort Report No. 23.

Ashton, D. and Green, F. (1996), *Education, Training and the Global Economy.* Cheltenham: Edward Elgar.

Atkinson, J. and Spilsbury, M. (1993), *Basic Skills and Jobs.* London: ALBSU.

Atkinson, J., Spilsbury, M. and Williams, M. (1993), *The Basic Skills Needed at Work: A directory.* London: ALBSU.

Barry, M. and Sutherland, R. (1999), *Achieving Core Zero: An Investigation into the Knowledge of Classical Algebra among Engineering Undergraduates at the University of Bristol.* Report available from the Graduate School of Education, University of Bristol.

Basic Skills Agency (1997), *International Numeracy Survey: A comparison of the Basic Numeracy Skills of Adults 16–60 in Seven Countries.* London: The Basic Skills Agency, 26.

Bates, I. (1998), 'The "empowerment" dimension in the GNVQ: a critical exploration of discourse, pedagogic apparatus and school implementation'. In A.D. Edwards (ed.), *Special Issue of Evaluation and Research in Education on Vocational Education*, 12, 1.

Boaler, J. (1993), 'The role of contexts in the mathematics classroom: do they make mathematics more "real"'. *For the Learning of Mathematics*, 13(2), 12–17.

Booth, L. (1984), *Algebra: Children's Strategies and Errors.* Windsor: NFER-Nelson.

Boudon, R. (1982), *The Unintended Consequences of Social Action.* London: Macmillan.

Brown, M. (1996), 'The context of the research – the evolution of the National Curriculum for mathematics'. In D. Johnson and A. Millett (eds), *Implementing the Mathematics National Curriculum, Policy, Politics and Practice.* London: Paul Chapman Publishing.

Brown, M. (1998), 'The tyranny of the international horse race'. In R. Slee and G. Weiner with S. Tomlinson (eds), *School Effectiveness for Whom? Challenges to the School Effectiveness and School Improvement Movements.* London: Falmer Press.

Brown, M. (1999), 'Problems of interpreting international comparative data'. In Jarworski, B. and Phillips, D. (eds), *Comparing Standards Internationally: Research and practice in mathematics and beyond.* Oxford: Symposium.

Bruner, J. (1996), *The Culture of Education.* Cambridge, MA: Harvard University Press.

Buckingham, D. (1999), 'Superhighway or road to nowhere? Children's relationships with digital technology'. *English in Education*, 33(1).

Bynner, J. and Parsons, S. (1997a), *It Doesn't Get Any Better: The Impact of Poor Basic Skills on the Lives of 37 year olds.* London: Basic Skills Agency.

Bynner J. and Parsons, S. (1997b), *Does Numeracy Matter?* London: Basic Skills Agency.

Bynner, J. and Parsons, S. (1998), *Use it or Lose it?* London: Basic Skills Agency.

Bynner, J. and Steedman, J. (1995), *Difficulties with Basic Skills.* London: Basic Skills Agency.

Bynner, J., Morphy, L. and Parsons, S. (1997), 'Women, employment and skills'. In Metcalf, H. (ed.), *Half our Future: Women, Skill Development and Training.* London: Policy Studies Institute.

Carey, S., Low, S. and Hansboro, J. (1997), *Adult Literacy in Britain.* London: The Stationery Office.

Channel 4 (Despatches) (1993), *All Our Futures: Britain's Education Revolution.* London: Channel 4 with the University of Manchester, Report to accompany the Channel 4 programme.

Cockcroft, W.H. (1982), *Mathematics Counts.* Report on the Committee of Inquiry into the Teaching of Mathematics. London: HMSO.

Cooper, B. (1998), 'Assessing National Curriculum mathematics in England: Exploring children's interpretation of Key Stage 2 tests in clinical interviews'. *Educational Studies in Mathematics*, 35(1), 19–49.

Cresswell, M. (1996), 'Defining, setting and maintaining standards in curriculum-embedded examinations: judgemental and statistical approaches'. In H. Goldstein and T. Lewis (eds), *Assessment: Problems, developments and statistical issues.* New York: Wiley.

Croft, A. (1999), 'Mathematical preparedness for entrance to undergraduate engineering degree programmes and diagnostic testing'. Paper presented at Gatsby seminar on Diagnostic Testing in Mathematics, Cambridge, April.

Dearden, L., Ferri, J. and Meghir, C. (1998), 'The effect of school quality on educational attainment and wages', Institute for Fiscal Studies Working Paper No. W98/3.

Dearing, R. (1996), *Review of Qualifications for 16–19 Year Olds.* London: SCAA.

Department for Education and Employment (DfEE) (1997), *Education Statistics.* London: The Stationery Office.

Department for Education and Employment (DfEE) (1998a), *Teacher Supply and Demand Modelling: A Technical Description.* London: The Stationery Office.

Department for Education and Employment (DfEE) (1997/1998b), *Statistics of Education: Teachers, England and Wales.* London: The Stationery Office.

Department for Education and Employment (DfEE) (1998c), *Teachers: Meeting the Challenge of Change.* London: The Stationery Office.

Department for Education and Employment (DfEE) (1999), *The National Numeracy Strategy: Framework for Teaching Mathematics from Reception to Year 6.* London: The Stationery Office.

Department of Education and Science (DES) (1985), *Mathematics from 5 to 16.* London: HMSO.

Department of Education and Science (DES)/Welsh Office (1988), *Advancing A Levels: Report of a Committee appointed by the Secretary of State for Education and Science and the Secretary of State for Wales (The Higginson Report)*. London: HMSO.

Dolton, P. (1990), 'The economics of teacher supply'. *Economic Journal*, 100, 91–104.

Dolton, P. and Vignoles, A. (1997), 'The impact of school quality on labour market outcomes', University of Newcastle upon Tyne Discussion Paper No. 97/03.

Dolton, P. and Vignoles, A. (1998), 'Reforming A levels: is a broader curriculum better?', Centre for Economic Performance and University of Newcastle upon Tyne, mimeo.

Dolton, P. and Vignoles, A. (1999), 'The economic case for A level reform', Centre for Economic Performance, London School of Economics, Discussion Paper No. 422.

Dowling, P., and Noss, R. (eds) (1990), *Mathematics versus the National Curriculum*. Basingstoke: Falmer Press.

Ekinsmyth, C. and Bynner, J. (1994), *The Basic Skills of Young Adults*. London: Basic Skills Agency.

Further Education Development Agency (FEDA), Institute of Education and The Nuffield Foundation (1995), *The Evolution of GNVQs: A National Survey Report*. London: FEDA.

Further Education Development Agency (FEDA), Institute of Education and The Nuffield Foundation (1997), *GNVQs 1993–1997: A National Survey Report*. London: FEDA.

Ferri, E. (ed.) (1993), *Life at 33: The Fifth Follow-up of the National Child Development Study*. London: National Children's Bureau and City University.

Fitz-Gibbon, C.T. (1985), 'A-level results in comprehensive schools: the COMBSE project, Year 1'. *Oxford Review of Education*, 11, 43–58.

Fitz-Gibbon, C.T. (1999), 'Long-term Consequences of Curriculum Choices with Particular Reference to Mathematics and Science'. *School Effectiveness and School Improvement*, 10, 1–16.

Fitz-Gibbon, C.T. and Vincent, L. (1994), *Candidates' Performance in Public Examinations in Mathematics and Science*. London: SCAA.

Fogelman, K. (ed.) (1983), *Growing Up in Great Britain*. London: Macmillan.

Further Education Funding Council (FEFC) (1994), *General National Vocational Qualifications in the Further Education Sector in England*. Report from the Inspectorate. Coventry: FEFC.

Further Education Unit (FEU), Institute of Education and The Nuffield Foundation (1994), *GNVQs 1993–1994: A National Survey Report*. London: FEU.

Goldstein, H. and Wolf, A. (1983), 'The report whose sum doesn't add up to much'. *Guardian*, 5 July.

Green, F. (1998), 'The value of skills'. *Studies in Economics*, University of Kent at Canterbury No. 98/19.

Green, A, Wolf, A and Leney, T. (1999), *Convergence and Divergence in European Education and Training Systems*. London: Institute of Education.

Hall, R. (1999), 'Following mathematical practices in design-oriented work'. In C. Hoyles, C. Morgan and G. Woodhouse (eds), *Rethinking the Mathematics Curriculum*. London: Falmer Press, 29–47.

Hansard (2000) 'Teacher Training'. In *House of Commons Written Answers for 20 March 2000*, pt 10, 10 April 2000, p. 2. (Available at www.parliament.the stationery-office.co.uk)

Harel, I. and Papert, S. (eds) (1991), *Constructionism*. Norwood, NJ: Ablex Publishing Corporation.

Harries, T. and Sutherland, R. (1999), 'Primary school mathematics text books: an international comparison'. In I. Thompson (ed.), *Issues in Teaching Numeracy in Primary Schools*. Buckingham: Open University Press.

Higher Education Statistics Agency (HESA) (1994/5–1997/8), *Students in Higher Education Institutions*. Cheltenham: HESA.

Higher Education Statistics Agency (HESA) (1994/5–1997/8), *First Destinations of Students Leaving Higher Education Institutions*. Cheltenham: HESA.

Howson, G., Harries, T. and Sutherland, R. (1999), *Primary School Mathematics Textbooks: An international study summary*. London: Qualifications and Curriculum Authority.

Hoyles C., Morgan, C. and Woodhouse, G. (eds) (1999), *Rethinking the Mathematics Curriculum*. London: Falmer Press.

Hoyles C., Newman, K. and Noss, R. 'Mind the Gap: Changing Expectations in University Mathematics'. Submitted article.

Hoyles C., Noss, R. and Pozzi, S. (1999), 'Mathematizing in practice'. In C. Hoyles, C. Morgan and G. Woodhouse (eds), *Rethinking the Mathematics Curriculum*. London: Falmer Press, 48–62.

Hoyles, C. (1997), 'The curricular shaping of students' approaches to proof'. *For the Learning of Mathematics*, 17(1), 7–15.

Hoyles, C. and Healy, L. (1999), 'Can they prove it?'. *Mathematics in School*, May.

Hughes, M., Desforges, C. and Mitchell, C. (2000), *Numeracy and Beyond: Applying Mathematics in the Primary School*. Buckingham: Open University Press.

Hunt, J. and Neunzert, H. (1994), 'Mathematics and industry'. In A. Joseph, F. Mignot, F. Murat, B. Priun and R. Reutschler (eds), *First European Congress of Mathematics*. Basel: Birkhäwer Verlag, 257–275.

Industry in Education (1997), *Towards Employability: Addressing the Gap between Young People's Qualities and Employer's Recruitment Needs, Report under the Chairmanship of Sir John Smith*. London: Industry in Education.

Institute for Public Policy Research (1990), 'A British Baccalaureat: Ending the division between education and training'. Education and Training Paper No. 1.

International Numeracy Survey (1997), *A Comparison of the Basic Skills of Adults 16–60 in Seven Countries*. London: Basic Skills Agency.

Jaworski, B. and Phillips, D. (eds) (1999), *Comparing Standards Internationally: Research and practice in mathematics and beyond*. Oxford: Symposium Books.

Kaput, J.J. and Roschelle, J. (1999), 'The mathematics of change and variation from a millennial perspective: new content, new context'. In C. Hoyles, C. Morgan and G. Woodhouse (eds), *Rethinking the Mathematics Curriculum*. London: Falmer Press, 155–170.

Keys, W., Harris, S. and Fernandes, C. (1996), *Third International Mathematics and Science Study: First National Report*. Slough: NFER.

Kieran, C. (1989), 'The early learning of algebra: a structural perspective'. In: J. Wagner and C. Keiran (eds), *Research Issues in the Learning and Teaching of Algebra*. Hillside: LEA.

Konold, C., Pollatsek, A., Well, A. and Gagnon, A. (1997), 'Students analyzing data: research of critical barriers'. In J.B. Garfield and G. Burrill (eds), *Research on the Role of Technology in Teaching and Learning Statistics: 1996 Proceedings of the 1996 IASE Round Table Conference*. Voorburg, The Netherlands: International Statistical Institute, 151–167.

Krueger, A. (1991), 'How computers have changed the wage structure: evidence from microdata, 1984–89'. Princeton University and NBER working paper.

Küchemann, D.E. (1981), 'Algebra'. In K. Hart (ed.), *Children's Understanding of Mathematics: 11–16*. London: John Murray.

Lave, J. (1988), *Cognition in Practice: Mind, Mathematics and Culture in Everyday Life*. Cambridge: Cambridge University Press.

Lew, H. (1999), 'New goals and directions for mathematics education in Korea. In C. Hoyles, C. Morgan and G. Woodhouse (eds), *Rethinking the Mathematics Curriculum*. London: Falmer Press, 218–227.

Lin Fou-Lai., Tsao Liang-Chi. (1999), 'Exam maths re-examined'. In C. Hoyles, C. Morgan and G. Woodhouse (eds), *Rethinking the Mathematics Curriculum*. London: Falmer Press, 228–239.

London Mathematical Society (LMS), Institute of Mathematics and its Applications, Royal Statistical Society (1995), *Tackling the Mathematics Problem*. London: LMS.

Masingila, J.O. (1993), 'Learning from mathematics practice in out-of-school situations'. *For the Learning of Mathematics*, 13(2), 18–22.

Mason, G. (1998), *Change and Diversity: The Challenges Facing Chemistry Higher Education*. London: Royal Society of Chemistry and Council for Industry and Higher Education.

Molyneux, S. and Sutherland, R. (1996*), Mathematics in GNVQ Science: The Case of Conversions*. Report to the Leverhulme Trust, Graduate School of Education. Bristol: University of Bristol.

Murnane, R.J., Willett, J.B. and Levy, F. (1995), 'The growing importance of cognitive skills in wage determination'. *Review of Economics and Statistics*, 77, 251–66.

National Assessment of Educational Progress (NAEP) (1983), Third National Mathematics Assessment. Denver: Education Commission of the States.

National Center for Education Statistics (NCES) (1997), *The Condition of Education*. Washington DC: NCES.

Noss, R. (1997), *New Cultures, New Numeracies*. Inaugural Lecture. London: Institute of Education.

Noss, R. and Hoyles, C. (1996), *Windows on Mathematical Meanings: Learning Cultures and Computers*. London, Boston: Kluwer Academic Publishers.

Noss, R., Healy, L. and Hoyles, C. (1997), 'The construction of mathematical meanings: connecting the visual with the symbolic'. *Educational Studies in Mathematics*, 33, 203–233.

Nunes, T., Schliemann, A.D. and Carraher, D.W. (1993), *Street Mathematics and School Mathematics*. Cambridge: Cambridge University Press.

Office for Standards in Education (OFSTED) (1994), *GNVQs in Schools: 1993–94: Quality and Standards of General National Vocational Qualifications*. London: HMSO.

Office for Standards in Education (OFSTED), Further Education Funding Council, and Training Standards Council (2000), *Pilot of New Key Skills Qualifications 1997–99*. London: OFSTED.

Organization for Economic Co-operation and Development (OECD) (1999), Thematic Review of the Transition from Initial Education to Working Life. USA Country Note. Paris: OECD.

Parsons, S. and Bynner, J. (1998), *Influences on Adult Basic Skills*. London: Basic Skills Agency.

Parsons, S. and Bynner, J. (1999), *Literacy, Leaving School and Jobs: The effect of poor basic skills on employment in different age groups*. London: Basic Skills Agency.

Prais, S. (1991), 'Vocational qualifications in Britain and Europe: theory and practice'. *National Institute Economic Review*, May, 86–92.

Prais, S.J. (1995), *Productivity, Education and Training*. Cambridge: Cambridge University Press.

Pratt, D. (1995), 'Young children's active and passive graphing'. *Journal of Computer Assisted Learning*, 11, 157–169.

Pringle, M.K., Butler, N. and Davies, R. (1986), *11,000 Seven Year Olds*. London: Longman, in association with National Children's Bureau.

Pryor, F.L. and Schaffer, D.L. (1999), *Who's not Working and Why*. Cambridge: Cambridge University Press.

Reynolds, D. and Muijs, D. (1999), 'Numeracy matters: Contemporary policy issues in the teaching of Mathematics'. In I. Thompson (ed.), *Issues in Teaching Numeracy in Primary Schools*. Buckingham: Open University Press.

Robinson, P. (1997), *The Myth of Parity of Esteem: Earnings and qualifications*. London: Centre for Economic Performance, London School of Economics. Working Paper No. 865.

Romberg, T.A. and Kaput, J.J. (1999), 'Mathematics worth teaching, mathematics worth understanding'. In E. Fennema and T.A. Romberg (eds), *Mathematics Classrooms that Promote Understanding*. New Jersey: Lawrence Erlbaum Associates, 3–17.

Roszak, T. (1986), *The Cult of Information: The Folklore of Computers and the True Art of Thinking*. Cambridge: Lutterworth Press.

Royal Society (1997), *Teaching and Learning Algebra pre-19. Report of a Royal Society/Joint Mathematical Council Working Group*. London: Royal Society.

Rudd, P. and Steedman, H. (1997), *GCSE Grades and GNVQ Outcomes*. London: Centre for Economic Performance, London School of Economics. Discussion Paper No. 366.

Schliemann, A. (1995), 'Some concerns about bringing everyday mathematics to mathematics education'. In L. Meira and D. Carraher (eds), *Proceedings of the Nineteenth Conference of the International Group for the Psychology of Mathematics Education*. Recife, Brazil, I, 45–60.

Schonell, F.J. and Cracknell, S.H. (1937), *Right from the Start Arithmetic Book 2*. London: Oliver and Boyd Limited.

School Curriculum and Assessment Authority (SCAA) (1996), *An Analysis of the 1995 GCE Results and Trends over Time*. London: SCAA.

School Curriculum and Assessment Authority (SCAA) (1997), *Literacy and Numeracy in the Workplace*. London: SCAA.

School Mathematics Project (SMP) (1984), *SMP 11–16*. Cambridge: Cambridge University Press.

Skills Task Force (1999), *Delivering Skills for All: Second Report of the National Skills Task Force*. London: Department for Education and Employment.

Southgate, V. (1962), *Southgate Reading Tests: Manual of Instructions*. London: University of London Press.

Steedman, H. and Hawkins, J. (1994), 'Shifting foundations: The impact of NVQs on youth training in the building trades'. *National Institute Economic Review*, 149, 93–101

Sutherland, R. (1995), 'Algebraic thinking – the role of computers'. In L. Burton and B. Jaworski (eds), *Technology and Mathematics Teaching: A bridge between teaching and learning*. Bromley: Chartwell Bratt.

Sutherland, R. (1998), *Mathematics Education, A Case for Survival*. Inaugural Lecture. Bristol: University of Bristol.

Sutherland, R. and Dewhurst, H. (1999) *Mathematics Education: Framework for Progression from 16–19 to HE*. Final report of a project funded by the Gatsby Technical Education Project. Bristol: University of Bristol. ISDN 0-86292-487-1.

Sutherland, R. and Pozzi, S. (1995), *The Changing Mathematical Background of Undergraduate Engineers*. London: The Engineering Council.

Teacher Training Agency (TTA) (1999), *Report of the Teacher Supply and Retention in London Project*. London: TTA.

University Grants Committee (1987–1988), *University Statistics 1987–1988: Students and Staff*. Universities Statistical Record.

Verschaffel, L., De Corte, E. and Borghart, I. (1996), 'Pre-service teachers' conceptions and beliefs about the role of real-world knowledge in arithmetic word problem solving'. In L. Puig and A. Gutiérrez (eds), *Proceedings of the Twentieth Conference of the International Group for the Psychology of Mathematics Education*. Valencia, Spain, IV, 387–394.

Vile, A. (1996), 'Development Semiotics: The evolution of a theoretical framework for the description of meaning-making in mathematics education and mathematics'. Unpublished PhD dissertation, South Bank University.

Wertsch, J. (1998), *Mind as Action*. Oxford: Oxford University Press.

Wolf, A. (1992), 'Mathematics for Vocational Students in France and England: Contrasting Provision and Consequences'. London: National Institute of Economic and Social Research: Discussion Paper No. 23.

Wolf, A. (1997), *The Tyranny of Numbers: An inaugural lecture*. London: Institute of Education.

Wolf, A. and Rapiau, M.-T. (1993), 'The academic achievement of craft apprentices in France and England'. *Comparative Education*, 29(1) 29–43

Wolf, A. and Steedman, H. (1998), 'Basic competence in mathematics: Swedish and English 16 year olds'. *Comparative Education*, 34(3), 241–259

Wood, A. (1994), *North–South Trade, Employment and Inequality*. Oxford: Clarendon Press.

Wood, D. (1998), *Overall Evaluations of the Integrated Learning Systems Evaluations*. Coventry: BECTA.

Name index

Adelman, C. 171
Ainley, J. 143, 144, 145, 147, 149, 152, 153
Arcavi, A. 75
Ashford, S. 62
Ashton, D. 135
Atkinson, J. 26

Barnett, C. 1
Barry, M. 75, 84, 97
Basic Skills Agency 28, 29, 68
Bates, I. 122
Boaler, J. 141
Booth, L. 95
Borghart, I. 141
Boudon, R. 114
Brown, M. 118
Bruner, J. 97, 98, 102
Buckingham, D. 162
Business and Technician Education Council 13, 107, 122, 123, 124, 126, 127
Bynner, J. 26, 28, 31, 37, 41, 42, 68, 69

Cambridge Training and Development Ltd 28
Carey, S. 26
Carraher, D.W. 146, 147
Channel 4 125, 132
City and Guilds 123, 124

Cockroft, W.H. 9, 10, 11, 13, 74, 76, 85, 88, 97, 98, 100, 138, 164, 165
Cooper, B. 142
Cracknell, S.H. 140
Croft, A. 81
Crowther Report 53

De Corte, E. 141
Dearden, L. 55
Dearing, R. 52, 53, 54, 55, 56, 57, 62, 66, 69, 126
Department for Education and Employment 57, 76, 90, 97, 99, 100, 121, 140, 141, 148, 154
Department of Education and Science 161
Desforges, C. 142
Dewhurst, H. 77
Dolton, P. 52, 71
Dowling, P. 11, 156

Ekinsmyth, C. 26, 28, 31, 42
Engineering Employers Federation 126
Economic and Social Research Council 174

Fernandes, C. 118, 158
Ferri, J. 55, 59

Fitz-Gibbon, C.T. 64, 66, 71, 113
French Ministry of Education 137
Further Education Development Agency 122, 127
Further Education Funding Council 127
Further Education Unit 107

Gagnon, A. 152
General Household Survey 59
Goldstein, H. 10
Gray, J. 62
Green, A. 12, 108, 131
Green, F. 67, 135

Hall, R. 166
Hansboro, J. 26
Harel, I. 169
Harries, T. 94
Harris, S. 118, 158
Hawkins, J. 124, 125, 131
Healy, L. 11, 157
Higher Education Statistics Agency 15, 16
Howson, G. 94
Hoyles, C. 3, 11, 155, 157, 163, 171, 172